C000102222

Horoscopes
2022

....

Aries

21 March – 20 April

igloobooks

igloobooks

Published in 2021
First published in the UK by Igloo Books Ltd
An imprint of Igloo Books Ltd
Cottage Farm, NN6 0BJ, UK
Owned by Bonnier Books
Sveavägen 56, Stockholm, Sweden
www.igloobooks.com

Copyright © 2021 Igloo Books Ltd

All rights reserved. No part of this publication may be
reproduced or transmitted in any form or by any means,
electronic, or mechanical, including photocopying, recording,
or by any information storage and retrieval system,
without permission in writing from the publisher.

0721 001
2 4 6 8 10 9 7 5 3 1
ISBN 978-1-80022-520-6

Written by Belinda Campbell and Denise Evans

Designed by Simon Parker
Edited by Natalie Graham

Printed and manufactured in China

CONTENTS

....

INTRODUCTION

This 15-month guide has been designed and written to give a concise and accessible insight into both the nature of your star sign and the year ahead. Divided into two main sections, the first section of this guide will give you an overview of your character in order to help you understand how you think, perceive the world and interact with others, and – perhaps just as importantly – why. You'll soon see that your zodiac sign is not just affected by a few stars in the sky, but by planets, elements and a whole host of other factors, too.

The second section of this guide is made up of daily forecasts. Use these to increase your awareness of what might appear on your horizon so that you're better equipped to deal with the days ahead. While this should never be used to dictate your life, it can be useful to see how your energies might be affected or influenced, which, in turn, can help you prepare for what life might throw your way.

By the end of these 15 months, these two sections should have given you a deeper understanding and awareness of yourself and, in turn, the world around you. There are never any definite certainties, but with an open mind you will find guidance for what might be, and learn to take more control of your own destiny.

THE CHARACTER OF THE RAM

· · · · · · · · · · · · · · · · · ·

First in the zodiac year, first to get up in the morning, first to lend a helping hand and probably first on school sports days; Arians are a bundle of magnetic energy and quick-fire ideas. They tend to be the charismatic leaders of their pack, even if they don't volunteer themselves for the job. Whatever adventure Arians choose to chase after, there will always be a queue of admiring followers turning to these lively trendsetters for inspiration. Arians are aspirational and unparalleled in their zest for life, creative ideas and ability to get what they want.

Born in spring at the start of the equinox, the life and energy of Arians is palpable. It germinates in their abundance of ideas, flowers in their extrovert behaviour and bursts into life through their sometimes-impulsive actions. For Arians, the beginning of any venture is where their excitement lives and, sadly, often also dies. Whilst Arians thrive on beginning projects, whether it's starting up a business or learning a new craft, they don't always have the patience to see it through, leaving a path of half-painted canvases, unfinished novels and dust-gathering roller skates in their wake. It's not that Arians are ones to give up as such, far from it, but their childlike energy and impulsiveness can often become an impatient restlessness if a certain endeavour isn't going their way as quickly as they'd like it to. When one has as many fantastic ideas as Arians do, it's easy to understand why they may choose to ditch one enterprise to pursue another newer and 'greener' one. Although this quick-burning fire of interest can be problematic in love for Arians, resulting in short-lived lusts, their dependability is generally what they are better known for. When a problem occurs and someone suggests 'I know a person who can help with that', that person is likely to be an Arian.

THE RAM

Despite being born in springtime, there's not too much that's lamb-like about Arians! The Ram is known for being headstrong, and uses its impressive horns to settle arguments until it finally wins. Arians do not like losing an argument and so rarely stop until they eventually win. It all comes back to being first because, as Arians would argue, what other outcome is there? This fighting quality has its pros and cons. Professionally, especially with those who are self-employed, the competitive, cardinal nature of Arians can be a vital characteristic for coming out top. It's important for Arians to be aware of their combative nature in their personal relationships, too. It's vital that they learn to identify when a win for someone else is equally a win for them. This will help to keep their relationships happy and long-standing. The Ram is wild, ruling and sometimes angry, and it's these shared qualities that can make Arians so alluring to others, and viewed as a challenge or a chore to keep up with.

MARS

It's probably no surprise that the fiery red planet of
Mars rules Aries. Named after the Roman god of war, Mars,
like the Aries sign, is often associated with passion and rage.
However, Arians, like war, can demonstrate strategy and
discipline just as much as they cause destruction and chaos.
Whilst Aries and Mars are closely linked to being red-hot and
ready to win a fight, there is more to both these parties than a
steamy appearance. Once past the attractive, bold-red of Mars,
it's key to note its comparatively small size in the solar system
and its proximity to Earth. These attributes make Mars known
as an inner or 'personal' planet. Similarly, whilst there may be
a lot to see on the surface of the charismatic, sociable side of
Arians, one might be mistaken for thinking that's all there is.
Despite being primarily extroverted, Arians tend to internalise
their deepest thoughts and feelings. They like to keep their
private lives just that, private. The apparent closeness but
inner mysteries of this planet and sign may be one of the
reasons why humankind is so captivated with the red planet
and Aries.

ELEMENTS, MODES
AND POLARITIES

Each sign is made up of a unique combination of three
defining groups: elements, modes and polarities. Each of these
defining parts can manifest themselves in good and bad ways
and none should be seen as a positive or a negative – including
the polarities! Just like a jigsaw puzzle, piecing these groups
together can help illuminate why each sign has certain
characteristics and help us find a balance.

ELEMENTS

Fire: Dynamic and adventurous, signs with fire in them can be extroverted. Others are naturally drawn to them because of the positive light they give off, as well as their high levels of energy and confidence.

Earth: Signs with the earth element are steady and driven with their ambitions. They make for a solid friend, parent or partner due to their grounded influence and nurturing nature.

Air: The invisible element that influences each of the other elements significantly, Air signs will provide much-needed perspective to others with their fair thinking, verbal skills and key ideas.

Water: Warm in the shallows and sometimes freezing as ice, this mysterious element is essential to the growth of everything around it, through its emotional depth and empathy.

MODES

Cardinal: Pioneers of the calendar, cardinal signs jump-start each season and are the energetic go-getters.

Fixed: Marking the middle of the calendar, fixed signs firmly denote and value steadiness and reliability.

Mutable: As the seasons end, the mutable signs adapt and give themselves over gladly to the promise of change.

POLARITIES

Positive: Typically extroverted, positive signs take physical action and embrace outside stimulus in their life.

Negative: Usually introverted, negative signs value emotional development and experiencing life from the inside out.

ARIES IN BRIEF

The table below shows the key attributes of Arians.
Use it for quick reference and to understand more about this fascinating sign.

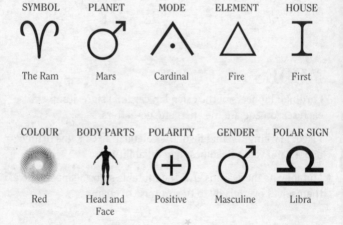

SYMBOL	RULING PLANET	MODE	ELEMENT	HOUSE
The Ram	Mars	Cardinal	Fire	First

COLOUR	BODY PARTS	POLARITY	GENDER	POLAR SIGN
Red	Head and Face	Positive	Masculine	Libra

ROMANTIC RELATIONSHIPS

· · · · · · · · · · · · · · · · · ·

Warm, devouring, dangerous and exciting, the Aries element of fire perfectly enlightens a potential spouse as to what the fast-burning love of an Arian can feel like. To some, the attraction of Arians is obvious, which is why there will often be a queue lining up. For others, the liveliness and spontaneity of Arians can be too hot to handle. The difficulty with finding someone that thinks the Arian free spirit is inspiring rather than tiring is perhaps why they are not best known for having long-term relationships. Arians can find the start of romantic relationships exciting but short-lived if they find themselves unmatched in passion and energy.

For a long-term relationship to work, Arians must continue to feel free – free to follow their ambitions, to act on their spontaneity and to roam where their hearts desire. A partner for an Arian is someone who will acknowledge the need for adventure, as well as the Arian desire for independence. It's essential for an Arian's partner to have separate interests, not only to keep the Arian satisfied but also to not lose themselves. Arians are cardinal, which means they initiate the zodiac calendar and commonly initiate their romantic relationships. When Arians hold a flame for someone, they do not make a secret of it and are quick to act.

Not everyone has the same energy and vigour as Arians; in fact, some pride themselves on being the best. So how can they find an equal? Is an Arian only suited to another Arian? Although some feel that fire can only be fought with fire, this obvious solution may not be the best partnership of elements.

11

Regardless of signs, what Arians appreciate in a partner is someone who challenges them, shows a desire to share in their passions and, most importantly, brings humour into their lives.

ARIES: COMPATIBILITY 3/5

When a fire sign meets fire, there is sure to be lots of heat between the two. Whilst this could make for an exciting start, which both partners are sure to relish, it may be that they burn too brightly together and end up scalding each other. Both masculine and fire signs, these two are likely to share characteristics like leadership and ambition and will encourage one another to achieve their full potentials. Whilst passions and interests are likely to be shared, two Rams could end up butting heads too frequently to form a harmonious romance.

TAURUS: COMPATIBILITY 3/5

The Bull and the Ram may look like two headstrong individuals doomed to clash, but they actually have the potential for a sensual relationship. Whilst their passions for each other are intense, this couple will need to keep a reign on their potential stubbornness and desire to win in order to form a lasting relationship outside of the sheets. The Taurean can be guilty of possessiveness, which the free-spirited Arian may struggle with. However, with a joint love of nature and being outdoors, this duo could find their paradise together.

GEMINI: COMPATIBILITY 4/5

Though very different in their approaches to relationships, these two positive signs can bring out the very best in one another. Communication is key for any relationship and the Geminian's talkative nature can help the Arian vocalise their dreams and ideas. These two can form an intellectual bond that lays a strong foundation for their love. The Twins and Ram are both guilty of starting projects and not finishing them, which can extend to their relationship with each other, but their similarities and positive natures are likely to still see them part as friends if the romance extinguishes.

CANCER: COMPATIBILITY 1/5

This pair shares opposite characteristics that don't always attract, sadly. A homely creature, the Cancerian may find the Arian's adventurous roaming too uncomfortable and unsettling. Conversely, the Arian will not thrive in this relationship if constricted or held back in any way by the Cancerian. However, these water and fire signs are true opposites, and therefore can stand to learn a great deal from one another. In particular, the Cancerian can teach the Arian to be more considered before acting, whilst the Arian can teach the Cancerian to be less worrisome.

LEO: COMPATIBILITY 2/5

Arians are used to being first, but they'll have to learn to share
the spotlight and decision-making if they fall for this leader
of the jungle. These two signs should clearly recognise their
similarities, and therefore know just how to advise and support
one another in reaching their goals. With the Leonian led
by the heart and the Arian by the head, arguments can be a
roaring battlefield when these two don't see eye to eye. Ego
and pride will need to be kept in check on both sides if this
relationship is to go the distance.

VIRGO: COMPATIBILITY 4/5

There's not a lot that's similar about how an Arian and
Virgoan think and approach their daily decisions. The Arian
rushes in excitedly to almost everything, whereas the
Virgoan needs to exhaust all the facts and options first. The
Arian can teach the Virgoan the benefits of not getting too
bogged down with decisions, and the Virgoan can teach the
Arian the equal importance of noticing the smaller details in
life. When these two team up, they will understand that they
are very, very different, and will likely admire those differences
in one another.

LIBRA: COMPATIBILITY 5/5

A polarity is complementary for any star-sign pairing. For an Arian, a Libran is the yin to their yang, the Sun to their Moon, the wind to their fire. Libra is an air sign, and can make the Arian's flames burn that much brighter. The Libran is best known for bringing harmony and balance into the world, and can make an ideal partner for the often-combative Arian. In this partnership of opposites, each can learn from the other in areas that they are lacking, with the Libran encouraging the Arian to communicate, and the Arian inspiring the Libran into action.

SCORPIO: COMPATIBILITY 2/5

If it's passion that an Arian desires in a relationship, Scorpio could be the perfect sign for romance. However, this match might be too combative for long-term happiness. Both ruled by the planet Mars, these two may come into this relationship armed and ready to fight. Scorpio's tendency to desire control of a situation could be a source of many explosive fights. If this fire and water sign can work out a balance of control and ease Scorpio's insecurities that, left unchecked, risk developing into jealousy, then they could have a steamy relationship rather than being left hot and bothered.

SAGITTARIUS: COMPATIBILITY 5/5

It will be a sure sign of Cupid's work if an Arian gets struck by one of the Sagittarian archer's arrows. This couple's compatibility is high due to their matching positivity and lively personalities. The Arian may have finally found their true match in the risk-taking Sagittarian. With a shared love of travel, there's unlikely to be any Arian adventure that the Sagittarian would pass up on. These two are go-getters and, if they can find shared interests, are an ideal match of two pioneering signs running off into the sunset together.

CAPRICORN: COMPATIBILITY 3/5

A Capricornian is not an obvious lover for an ambitious Arian, but shouldn't necessarily be ruled out entirely as a potential partner. The Capricornian usually takes much longer to size up a partner than the quick-working Arian, so patience will need to be exerted if this challenging relationship is to work. Like with any partnership in life, their differences can become their strengths. They should, however, be mindful of not wanting to change one another. Instead, the Capricornian and Arian should strive to make the other a better, more well-rounded person.

AQUARIUS: COMPATIBILITY 3/5

Two signs known for their admirable quality of being a good friend to all, an Arian and Aquarian should have a good solid foundation of friendship to base their romantic relationship on. This coupling of air and fire will always make for a fuelled relationship. Independence is key for keeping the Aquarian lover happy, so the Arian should be careful with trying to control the relationship or forcing the Aquarian to commit too soon. Whilst these two signs have many things in common, it will be discovering each other's differences that will be essential in keeping both partners interested in this relationship.

PISCES: COMPATIBILITY 2/5

A dreamy Piscean and action-lead Arian can learn a lot from one another, if they can find the impetus to do so. The Piscean often fears delving into the deep end of desires, generally choosing to back other's dreams over their own. The Arian will want to help the Piscean reach their full potential, but may unintentionally upset their extremely sensitive lover. However, the Piscean can use the same emotional side to offer much-needed support to the Arian, who often forgets to pause for thought. Together, they could form a considered connection, deeper than most.

FAMILY AND FRIENDS

· · · · · · · · · · · · · · · · ·

Born in the first house of the zodiac calendar, symbolising the self and personality, Arians are known for their individuality. So where does that leave their family and friends? Arians love to offer both practical and physical support; putting up a shelf, booking a house viewing, mowing the lawn, getting people out of bed for marathon training (that they may or may not have signed everyone up for!). Arians are first to help others, and can be extremely encouraging and invested in seeing those closest to them realise goals. Family and friends will appreciate having Arians in their lives and acknowledge the positive influence they bring.

As siblings, Arians can be aspirational figures that their brothers and sisters look up to. This idolisation can manifest itself in numerous ways, such as copying their hairstyles or borrowing their clothes. Just be sure to ask Arians first before taking their things to avoid sparking their temper. Should Arians wish to start their own family and have children of their own, their approach to parenting will be fun and energetic. Arians will have no problem running around after young children, keeping up with their endless energy and behaving like big kids themselves. The ever-changing demands of parenthood would likely suit Arians by keeping them challenged, whilst satisfying their childlike and curious nature.

Arians do well in polar relationships, where others supply traits in which they themselves are lacking. However, what might be most important for any successful bond with Arians is having common interests. Sport is likely to be an area where Arians have hobbies, and they will often meet friends this way.

FAMILY AND FRIENDS

Whether it's joining a sports club or competing in events, Arians' love for physical hobbies will steer them towards finding people with similar interests.

Another key characteristic of Arians is their need for freedom. This craving for independence will mean that travel is usually prevalent, whether it is for work or pleasure. This love of travel can mean that Arians have a far-reaching global network of family and friends. If Arians find that their work takes them away, it's key to seek close friendships where both sides have a strong sense of independence and will not feel abandoned. Life-loving Sagittarians and individualist Aquarians can make the best family and friends for any fast-paced Arians.

Friends of Arians will know that they are always in, whatever the plan. Their enthusiasm is instant and uplifting. Arians aren't likely to decline offers of fun, which can prove troublesome when they later realise they have double-booked themselves – again. Beware of being bumped to the rejection list if an Arian finds a better offer elsewhere. It's nothing personal. Arians often cancel plans without thinking they may be upsetting friends and family by doing so.

MONEY AND CAREERS

· · · · · · · · · · · · · · · · ·

Being a particular star sign will not dictate certain types of career, but it can help identify potential areas for thriving in. To succeed in the workplace, it is just as important to understand strengths and weaknesses to achieve career and financial goals.

Arians are driven more by goals than money, which for some individuals may be one and the same, but in most cases will overlap in some ways. When someone succeeds in their professional field, which Arians generally do, being a high earner usually comes with the territory. So even if money was not the end goal for Arians, it is usually a by-product of success and passion.

Arians are typically competitive and overflowing with energy, which, if channelled at an early age, can make sports an obvious career path. Some Arians prefer the competition and sociability of team sports, and may choose to follow in the footsteps of many famous Arian footballers. Other Arians prefer the constant competition of self-improvement and find running a more satisfactory sport – just like Olympic gold medallist, Mo Farah.

Arians are self-starters. This go-getter initiative may materialise itself as a crowdfunding project, a hobby that turns into a business idea, or a mini side project that turns into a profitable company. Whatever career ladder Arians climb, they will scale it quickly and always reach the top of their profession. That is, of course, as long as the job at hand is able to satisfy their ambition, and Arians can see that their frequent ideas are being listened to and acted upon.

A job in which Arians feel stagnant or stifled is not one they will stay in for any great length of time. Arians work best when they have freedom, be it creatively or by working flexible hours, and may struggle to satisfy this need for independence in more traditional workplaces. Self-employment options may be a better fit for this me-first sign, allowing them to be their own boss, dictate their own hours and free themselves from the nine to five.

In a modern world of online influencers, such as Arians Casey Neistat and Zoe Sugg, the sky's the limit for pioneering individuals who aren't afraid to go after what they want. This digital age is perhaps the most exciting era for Arians, as it has given them an outlet that lets them work nomadically from coffee shops or mountaintops.

If drawn to a more traditional workspace, the me-first attitude will need to be dialled down. Lessening the need to constantly win and learning to be able to compromise is essential learning for Arians if they are to thrive – which fundamentally is what they want! That being said, any team that contains one or more Arians is likely to come out on top. Arians are practical problem-solvers and are first to help colleagues find the best solutions. This makes them generally very popular and an asset to any company.

As with family, colleagues cannot be chosen. Therefore, it can be advantageous to use star signs to learn about their key characteristics and discover the best ways of working together. Geminians can make for a helpful colleague by encouraging Arians to see a project from an alternative viewpoint. Geminians are also champion communicators, and can connect to Arians on an intellectual level and help them verbalise their ideas. Arians share a desire of winning with their fire sign relation, Leo. However, just like close families, these two know how to fight better than anyone and can make for argumentative teammates. As with any successful relationship, Arians should try to exercise patience and take a leaf out of the Geminian book about how best to communicate with colleagues or customers in order to thrive in professional endeavours.

HEALTH AND WELLBEING

Arians are known for being one of the strongest and healthiest signs in the zodiac calendar. All associations with this sign, lively fire plus combative Mars mixed with the headstrong Ram, can equate to the makings of an energetic individual. It's important that Arians find ways of positively expelling this natural energy and one of the ways this can be done effectively is through sports. Arians are unlikely to be satisfied simply by running out their energy on a treadmill in the gym, rather this sign is more likely to enjoy team sports such as football or basketball to complement their social and competitive nature. Other Arians that feel the ruling of Mars more keenly may find that martial arts are their passion, like fellow Arian Jackie Chan.

Represented by the zodiac symbol of the Ram, this headstrong animal perfectly symbolises the ferocity and wildness in which Arians charge after what they desire most. The Ram is known not only for its strength, but also for having unbelievable balance on dizzyingly high and rocky terrains. This may be why some Arians find that their sense of adventure leads them to try thrill-seeking sports that rely on strength and balance, such as rock climbing, mountain biking or even aerial acrobatics. Whether Arians focus their abundance of energy and aptitude for action into a particular sport, their love for adventure is likely to have them craving after some sort of lifestyle in the great outdoors, whether that's hiking or wild swimming.

Physical activity is well suited to Arians, not only for the obvious benefits of keeping their bodies physically healthy, but also for their mental wellbeing. This highly charged sign needs a positive outlet for releasing their excess energy.

If Arians feel a fight boiling up in them, they would do well to throw their trainers on, step out of their front door into some fresh air and just run it out. Chances are they'll feel much better for having expelled some of their energy, especially applying it to something constructive, as this is what this positive sign naturally craves.

It's key for Arians to stay active in an area that brings them joy so as to avoid frustration, but this sign should be wary of pushing themselves too much and too quickly, as they could end up injuring themselves in the process. Slowing down, weighing up risks and taking a moment to simply breathe can help Arians maintain a positive state of mind. They would do well to try incorporating more meditative hobbies into their active lifestyles. Yoga will help stretch out overworked muscles and mediation will help calm a warrior-like approach to life, and bring a much-needed breath of tranquillity. Arians are traditionally linked to the head, and may find that they suffer from headaches more acutely and frequently, or conversely not at all. Either way, if Arians can periodically pause and calm their active mind and body, they could find it brings a clearer focus that leads to long-term health and happiness.

Aries

....

DAILY FORECASTS
for 2021

OCTOBER

· · · · · · · · · · · · · · · · ·

Friday 1st

On the whole, you feel well balanced and outgoing. Optimism fills you and you can express your desires to a loved one. This may not be the same at work, pesky Mercury is squaring off with Pluto and causing trouble in the workplace with close acquaintances. Stick to the rules today.

Saturday 2nd

If you feel compelled to tell someone a secret, beware of who you choose to share it with. Amorous Venus is in a sector that deals with taboo so could manipulate you into sharing more than you intended. You may be digging a big hole, which will be troublesome to climb out of.

Sunday 3rd

Getting ready for Monday by checking your to-do list is the flavour of the day. There may be a list of Sunday chores needing your attention. Friends and lovers want your time, but this is not possible today. Do the right thing and see to the daily grind.

Monday 4th

The week starts on a good foot and you are feeling serious and work-orientated. You have no time for daydreams or spiritual stuff today. Surprise yourself and expend some nervous energy at the gym or work flat out on a project. Nothing will go unchecked today.

Tuesday 5th

Lovely energy comes in this afternoon and you let yourself relax. A lover may seduce you, but in a gentle way. There is a great balance between you and a partner. You are looking after yourself better these days. Time spent with another or spoiling yourself is time well spent.

Wednesday 6th

Today, there is a new moon in your relationship sector. This will meet up with your ruler, Mars, making you activate something new in relating. You can be quite assertive now. Later, the Moon meets Mercury retrograde in the same sector; make sure everyone is on the same page to avoid upsets with important people.

Thursday 7th

Pluto is now direct and you will feel less like people are coaxing you out of your comfort zone. Venus enters your travel sector and will help you taste the delights of foreign lands. Ideas for studying different cultures or religions will come to you. This is worth exploring.

Friday 8th

Your ego and energy are on fire right now. This weekend you will be filled with adrenalin and possibly initiate several projects at once. You must play by the rules and not go expecting too much from someone. They may not have the same goals as you.

Saturday 9th

Make a fluid agenda for the day. The planetary action is extreme. Your love life may be disrupted or totally silent. Mercury is speaking to Mars and they both want action they are not going to get. This has you looking back and yearning for the past when, allegedly, life was easier.

Sunday 10th

Saturn now goes direct. Any obstructions you may have felt in your social circle will ease off and you will see them as important lessons. Other connections to the Moon are easy, giving you a cooperative time with a lover or other special person.

Monday 11th

You are outgoing and optimistic as you start the week. Travel plans have been on your mind, but you are yet to make anything concrete. This distracts you from your work somewhat, but does not interfere with it. Keep up that good cheer. As a fire sign, it suits you.

Tuesday 12th

Ideas flow and your neural pathways light up constantly. You should impress all your work colleagues with efficiency today. It will be easy to climb that corporate ladder with all eyes watching. Performing under pressure seems like a walk in the park. Just don't let it go to your head.

Wednesday 13th

Nice energy and your good mood continue to make this week fly by. You may have to bring something to a natural end or scrub it clean and make it new. Allow yourself to dream a little now and get out the travel brochures. There could be an educational trip waiting for you.

Thursday 14th

The Moon drifts into your social sector and meets with newly direct Saturn. You get the first pat on your back for discerning false friends from true ones. A little niggle in your social groups can muddy the water, but you should now know how to deal with this graciously.

Friday 15th

Are you ready for the weekend? Once again, you fill with joy and look forward to time with friends. This could be with online groups, too. Your leadership qualities may be called on now and this makes you feel important. Watch that ego, you don't need it stroked.

Saturday 16th

Today, if you do not feel like being sociable, you should stay home and switch off. You could have a crisis of conscience and decide that you need to spend more time on spiritual matters. Yoga and meditation attract you and finding a spiritual tribe means more to you now.

Sunday 17th

Jupiter joins the party and turns direct in your social sector. This is a great help as he is associated with spiritual teachers and the search for truth. You spend time in meditation or simply thinking about things in a brand-new way. Prepare for a new download.

. . . .

Monday 18th

Mercury also goes direct in your relationship sector. You feel this shift as it is a more personal one. You now need to talk directly to lovers or important partners. The Moon in your sign helps you to be assertive and kind. Now is the time to initiate new projects.

Tuesday 19th

The planets are all saying that you are good to go. Travel and spiritual matters can be communicated now. Say what is in your heart with full expression. Your ruler gets a good luck charm for you from lucky Jupiter. Get a game plan and make a start.

Wednesday 20th

You might feel resistant or hesitant to put your plans in action today. This will pass quickly. A full moon in your sign is all the permission you need. Look back at the last six months at how your intentions have manifested. Have the planetary retrogrades taught you something valuable?

Thursday 21st

The weekend has not begun yet, but you will consider an evening out. Is this because you are avoiding a task that needs doing? You act like a child today if you cannot get your own way. Do your chores and the reward will be much sweeter.

Friday 22nd

Lovers may cause tension as their needs clash with your career priorities. Business partners or people you have joint financial interests with also take up much of your time. You must bring closure to any ties you have with another that are no longer valid or useful. This may upset someone close to you.

Sunday 31st

A calmer Sunday has you tidying up, decluttering and checking in with your health. Jobs on your to-do list are more easily completed, bringing satisfaction. You enjoy the thought of getting things in order before the working week begins again. There may even be time to go to the gym today.

NOVEMBER
. . . .

Monday 1st
Ideas flood into your head today. There is no time for clouded
thinking or emotion, it is all about clarity and vision. Relations
with lovers or partners are favoured under the influence of
Mercury and good luck planet, Jupiter. Conversations are
uplifting and optimistic.

Tuesday 2nd
Mercury is squaring off with Pluto today. This could mean
that lovers and co-workers clash now. Both require your
attention. A balancing moon in your relationship sector will
help you to deal with this in a manner that suits all. Try not
to be manipulated.

Wednesday 3rd
An emotional heart-to-heart with someone close will help
to prevent any subtle power games going on. You must be
firm but fair to avoid any misunderstandings. You have lucky
Jupiter on your side so use him well. Look for the truth, the
justice and the balance in any conflict.

Thursday 4th
The Moon slips into your intimacy sector. Sex, death, rebirth
and shared finances will be up for review. A new moon today
in this sector urges the need to make intentions and goals in
these areas. Aggression and restriction may block your path
forward for now. Stick with it, as this will soon ease.

Friday 5th

Be careful today, as exposure is the theme. Fools, liars and
cheats are in the firing line, so make sure you are not one
of them. Mercury and Venus both shift signs. He goes to the
underworld of your psyche and she becomes the boss.
Fairness and equality in the workplace will be investigated.

Saturday 6th

Easy energy gives you a quiet Saturday. Private investigations
are not urgent but occupy your mind over the weekend. This
could simply be that you have found something you wish to
learn about and now have the time to study. Skills learned in
the past are useful now.

Sunday 7th

Your dream life seems to have gone askew lately. Tangible duties
and experiences seem more important. This might niggle you
somewhat and compel you to rethink your future travel plans.
Do not fear; the impulse to follow your dreams will return.

Monday 8th

Your obligations and responsibilities take up your mind space
as the working week begins. Your energy is on top form.
Communication, compassion and assertiveness all go a long
way to make this a day you are praised for your efficiency at
work. Enjoy this energy; you deserve it.

Tuesday 9th

You need to look at something from a different perspective today. Either your opinion or the thing itself needs to be transformed. There is gold to be found here but the lead is all that is showing. Do some investigating and find the worth in something you are almost ready to discard.

Wednesday 10th

Very heavy energy from the Moon, Mercury and Mars makes this quite an intense day. Heated discussions are very likely. Mars and Mercury are both mining for information in your intimacy sector so this will involve lovers. Saturn makes his presence very obvious and reminds you to respect boundaries.

Thursday 11th

Social groups including activism can create hostility today. Protest marches and petitions might stir up some problems. Closer to home, you may fall out with friends who have high opinions of themselves. A day of unrest where anything could happen and probably will.

Friday 12th

Retreat for the weekend. The Moon has landed in your dreams sector and you long to be alone with your thoughts and personal visions. Venus connects nicely to the Moon lending you beauty, balance and harmony. Your thoughts can go quite deep today; the mysteries of life fascinate you.

Saturday 13th

Meditation or yoga are the best things you can do today. Enjoy peace and stillness and try to clear your mind. If this is not possible, surrender to whatever comes to you and see where it leads. You may surprise yourself as something from your unconscious comes up for healing.

Sunday 14th

Are you receiving messages from the divine? You may think it is a creation of your own mind but nevertheless, it is something you can work with. Pluto asks that you change something for the better. By afternoon, you are feeling yourself again as the Moon enters your sign.

Monday 15th

You will feel as if nothing is going right for you today. The two luck bringing planets, Venus and Jupiter, are squaring off with Moon and Sun. Ego and emotions must be put to one side or you will feel this intensely. Saturn is watching to see how far you can go without breaking.

Tuesday 16th

An altercation at work may prove challenging, but you will come off the winner. Stay strong and use your powers of persuasion. Do not let your emotions get the better of you. Changes will be made but they will be worth it and will bring you good fortune.

Wednesday 17th

The Moon moves into your money sector today and you will be looking at how you value almost everything in your life. Consider how authority figures have shaped you this year. What strengths have you gained? Electrically charged energy around finances gets things moving or changing today.

Thursday 18th

Neptune sees to it that your mind and emotions both have attachments that need dissolving. Uranus gets in on the act, too, by sitting with the Moon in your money sector. More shake-ups regarding money and value are likely now. Do not resist, this is a necessary change.

Friday 19th

A full moon in your money sector illuminates just how much things have changed here. You may have invested with another and can now see if it was worth it. This afternoon, communications with siblings may offer good advice and encouragement. A nice surprise awaits you as a reward.

Saturday 20th

Everybody wants to give you their opinion today. There are nuggets of wisdom to be had if you discern wisely. Otherwise, the mental chatter can be too much for you and overwhelm your mind. Friends mean well but today it is best to say thank you and retreat in order to process all that information.

Sunday 21st

Your brain feels full of fog today. There is nothing you can do to gain clarity and this frustrates you. Use the rest of the weekend to switch off with meditation, a walk in nature or a good book. You will not see clearly until the Moon passes its connection to Neptune.

Monday 22nd

Visits to family or a maternal figure can soothe your over-wrought brain today. Go to someone where you can be yourself and be nurtured. A loving connection between Venus and Mars means that work and passion combine well. The Sun now warms up your travel sector and revitalises that urge.

Tuesday 23rd

You feel that you would like to spend more time in the comfort of your own home or that of a parent's today. Like a child, you resist grown-up life and its responsibilities. This is OK; just do not let it be seen in the workplace.

Wednesday 24th

Mercury is done investigating the depths of your psyche and has now left for foreign lands. Anything he may have triggered now needs to be healed. You may have some conflict with an authority figure in the workplace today. Speak your truth with courage, compassion and kindness for all.

Thursday 25th

Is there someone in your social circle whom you greatly admire? Today, they may challenge you to think about personal boundaries once again. Thoughts about skills learned in the past come up and maybe there is now a need for them to be put to good use.

Friday 26th

Another leader or authority figure challenges you. Your own leadership skills are questioned, and you have to justify yourself. If you are in any way emotional about this, you will not get very far. You must make yourself seen and heard without having a tantrum.

Saturday 27th

Today you must get things in order. A tidy office or home will help you think more clearly. This is a time to wind things down or think about completing projects already started. What is hanging around that is no longer needed or not doing you any good?

Sunday 28th

Neptune wants to whisk you away to fantasy land, but you are advised not to go there. The best thing to do with this energy is to have a scented salt bath. Adding bad habits and unhealthy coping mechanisms to the mix will make you too far to reach when you're needed. Try to stay grounded.

Monday 29th

Mercury is in the heat of the Sun and has nothing to say, your job is to listen. Your ruler is in connection to Neptune and is also urging you to take action with your dreams. This is conflicting energy, so listen for messages and directions showing whether to act or be still.

Tuesday 30th

Today you feel more outgoing and wish to connect with a partner. Dreams and boundaries can be merged now, making today great for romantic shared visions. Work may be a stick in the mud, but this can be avoided or dealt with easily. Plan those future trips now.

DECEMBER

. . . .

Wednesday 1st

Neptune turns direct today and any illusions you have harboured in recent months should dissolve. Clear-sighted dreams will now be more realistically attainable. You have an urge to delve deep and luck will be on your side. Great discoveries are possible now.

Thursday 2nd

Consider your limits and stretch yourself today. This may cause you discomfort but will help you grow. Remember what a caterpillar must go through to become a butterfly. A nice connection between the Moon and Venus helps make the workplace happy today. There will be more harmony between the workers and those in charge.

Friday 3rd

A boost of energy from your ruler, Mars, makes you more outgoing and extroverted. Watch that this does not rattle someone in charge. Keep your drive low key but do not stifle it. Today you need to spread your wings and look over the horizon.

Saturday 4th

A new moon in your travel sector helps you to put vacation or higher education plans into action. Seek information and research adventures you wish to take. You will know if this is realistic or not, but either way you can still dream. Make an action plan of small achievable goals.

Sunday 5th

You are responsible and considerate today. Your mind is brought back to considering how to climb the mountain of your vision. It may seem huge at the moment. Keep your head out of the clouds until you are at the summit and the view makes you feel proud. You can do this.

Monday 6th

All the outer planets are connecting to the Moon in your career sector today. The helpful connections help you to see the bigger picture and where your seemingly small part in it is. Change the world or just yourself one step at a time. You will surpass yourself.

Tuesday 7th

This morning, the Moon meets up with the planet of permanent change and will aid you in bringing closure to something no longer useful. By afternoon, your vision is still very much in your line of sight. You may seek advice from close friends or online interest groups to spur you on.

Wednesday 8th

A friendly teacher or inspirational person is worth talking to, today. You might butt heads in a radical conversation, but this is meant to get you thinking. Discussing subjects that are outside the box will get your motor running ready for the big journey ahead of you.

Thursday 9th

Any conflict today is likely to be blown out of proportion. Alternatively, your energy could be so great that you burn the candle at both ends or run a marathon. Try to slow down in the afternoon and get ready for a dreamy weekend.

Friday 10th

You may connect with others who are spiritual today. Your mood is changeable, and you are open to new ideas. If yoga or meditation is your thing, then time spent on these will be beneficial. Empathy is strong and friends may seek you out to cry on your shoulders. Allow them the space.

Saturday 11th

A Saturday retreat with a good book or a group of like-minded people will calm you today. Dreams and visions take you to your own inner world and get you looking at things from a different perspective. Listen to your inner voice while there, what is it saying?

Sunday 12th

Venus and Pluto meet up today in your career sector. This can be manipulative energy and you will need to watch out amongst certain people. It can also be that you make a big change which will bring great pleasure. Another aspect is that a love affair could end or be transformed.

Monday 13th

Mercury now enters your career sector. He deals with trade and commerce so use him wisely while he is here. Business talks will be more frequent and deals can be signed. Mars also shifts, marching into your travel sector and stepping up his game with your plans to explore new territory.

Tuesday 14th

You may have trouble with feminine or maternal energy today, particularly if it is associated with the workplace. You may feel belittled, or as if a co-worker or someone in authority is trying to undermine your efforts. Use your words kindly today, keep your integrity and do not fall to backstabbing or gossip.

Wednesday 15th

Boundaries get breached today. They may be yours or another's and this will cause unrest. You might feel emotionally drained and rely on conditioning and old habits to get you through the day. This will pass quickly, so don't dwell on it – it's not worth it.

Thursday 16th

Today has a better energy attached. Harmony is restored in the workplace and any changes made are easily implemented. This is a change for the better as you will see when you think about it. Don't let someone with an overinflated ego take over any of your social group activities.

Friday 17th

There is a lot you need to communicate or take time to process today. This may make you irritated as it's probably not what you want to be doing. You are revved up for the weekend but there are jobs that need completion and people to contact before you can relax.

Saturday 18th

Venus goes retrograde today. This is a period of time where love affairs can end or someone from you past will reappear. To help make this better for you, set your mind to work and your responsibilities. Duty, and whatever pays the bills, comes first.

Sunday 19th

Today, there is a full moon in your communications sector. Along with Venus newly in retrograde, this will highlight how you think, speak and listen to people in authority. You may have been in two minds about a situation or person, but now you will receive clarification. This could also bring some relief.

Monday 20th

The Moon is now in your family sector and you have the need to hunker down and surround yourself with the familiar and comfortable. You are in the mindset for a working week and this can cause some tension in the workplace. Use this time to process new ideas.

Tuesday 21st

The winter solstice is here and the shortest day may be
a little depressing. Keep allowing yourself to feel comforted
by nurturing people and eating nourishing foods. A festive
family meal will appease those needs. The winter ahead of
you does not need to be long and dark; it can be warm
and cosy.

Wednesday 22nd

You are able to express yourself well today. Stand in the
limelight and appreciate the glow. You might rub someone up
the wrong way, but this is not your fault. You have fiery energy
and need to burn it off today. Be creative and loving, and let
your inner child play.

Thursday 23rd

Jupiter sits at the final degree of your social sector. His year-long
stay here has shown you who are true friends and gurus, and you
may have found your soul group. This critical degree asks that
you make sure all is in order in this area before he moves on.

Friday 24th

This is a busy time for all and the planets are showing this. Go
at your own pace and get the chores done. You feel a duty to
help and do more than your fair share today. There will be power
struggles and tension. Take the pressure off elders in the family.

Saturday 25th

Christmas is here and brings nice surprises, but also the usual
annoyances. You may not have time to relax and enjoy the day.
The first effect of Venus retrograde will be evident today with her
meet up with Pluto. This can be controlling or transforming.

Sunday 26th

There is softer energy today after yesterday's rush. You are more likely to kick back and put your feet up. Relationships go well and conversations will range from loving responsibility to the mildly ridiculous. Have fun with family games and silliness. Laughing and dreaming go hand-in-hand today.

Monday 27th

A balancing moon energy sees that you get your own needs met while also seeing to the needs of others. Important people such as partners appreciate your efforts today. Much can get done in good spirits. You remember personal boundaries, which is important while Venus is in retrograde.

Tuesday 28th

The energy shifts and makes for a day of misunderstandings. A bossy person may upset you today. It might be a good idea to step way from it all and have some alone time. You will be deep in thought in the evening as bigger life issues take you away from the mundane and small talk.

Wednesday 29th

Jupiter, the luck-bringer, steps into your sector of dreams and spirituality. As a guru or preacher figure, you will notice that you reach out more to connect with the divine in the next year. You will feel this as a big push and it will unsettle you.

Thursday 30th

Mercury meets Pluto today and they talk about the gold hidden in your psyche. Something inside you is ready to come up for healing now. You have what it takes to do some introspection and follow the necessary paths to do your soul work. Well done; you can do this.

Friday 31st

On the last day of 2021, you look back at what worked and what did not. You are emotionally driven towards your goals now. There is an attachment to these that you do not want to let go of. Enjoy any get-togethers tonight. You will bring fun to the party.

Aries

....

DAILY FORECASTS
for 2022

JANUARY
· · · · · · · · · · · · · · · · · ·

Saturday 1st

Happy New Year and welcome to 2022. If you're setting new year goals, you may feel conflicted. A need to get out and explore the wider world is at odds with your need to look inside yourself. Think about the long-term gains before making decisions. Spontaneity needs a measure of restraint.

Sunday 2nd

A new moon suggests that you have the capability and potential to improve your career. If this can be combined with travel opportunities, all the better. Social and shared interest groups will receive a boost now and there may be a leadership role for you here too. Get networking and see what is out there for you.

Monday 3rd

You may feel power struggles or control issues arising in the workplace. A person or issue from the past may have reappeared and upset the status quo. Sit tight as this can be worked through fairly. You may find that you're already forming connections with your wider community.

Tuesday 4th

If you must say what is on your mind, be sure that it is honest and kind. This could be a day where unnecessary gossip or hurtful comments get out of control. Pull back and refrain from getting involved if this is possible. Take responsibility for your part.

Wednesday 5th

You have the right mind and energy to achieve something today. This could be related to a new project or responsibility within your groups. You may also be attracted to long-distance travel or learning something new. Follow where this energy is taking you. It may be good to broaden your horizons.

Thursday 6th

Turn inwards today as you may wish to do some introspection or self-evaluation. This may feel challenging at first as there are no instant results. However, in your solitude, you may come up with ideas that can change your fortune and this gives you more optimism for the coming year.

Friday 7th

Tap into your true north and ask yourself what it is that you need to be aligned with. Seek out activities or future paths that feel right and true. This may become more apparent as the year evolves. You may be able to process awkward feelings about work and power.

Saturday 8th

Be sociable today and get networking and connecting with like-minded folk. You may discover a whole new tribe who can help you advance your own agenda. Make yourself available to wider groups and see what can be exchanged to benefit all involved. Altruism can be one of your strengths now.

Sunday 9th

Problems with manipulation tactics may surface. Be careful that your energy doesn't get attached to this as it could tarnish your reputation. Your responsibility is to step back and observe how this plays out. Fairness and harmony are not easily reached today. Don't force any issues and keep a low profile.

Monday 10th

This is a tense time, but it will pass. It's how you respond that is the key. Take some time to assess what is valuable to you and if there is enough quality in your life. Superficial will not do now. Aim higher than necessary and anything less should gratify.

Tuesday 11th

The planetary energy is somewhat unstable today. You may feel a little lost and unfocused. Be still and observe where your attention goes. It may be that your physical energy doesn't match or align with your true north. Are you heading in the right direction? Take a rest.

Wednesday 12th

You may be feeling much better today. Your self-control is good and it's showing you in a good light in the workplace. Beginnings and endings, or transformations that feel right for you, can enhance your self-esteem. You may have taken the first steps on your personal journey for this year.

Thursday 13th

Mercury turns retrograde tomorrow, so use today to prepare. Have important conversations this morning and back up all devices. Communications will need to be crystal clear or risk trouble. Your online and social groups could be on the verge of something big but may have to wait until retrograde is over.

Friday 14th

You could be feeling challenged today and may need some time alone. Conversations may drain you or feel restricting. If you detect that something is dragging you off-course, hold tight as this is temporary. There is a need for you to be direct in all your communications now.

Saturday 15th

Exhaustion is possible today if you insist on pushing against the tide. This may make you feel vulnerable or useless. Retreat to your home and safety zone. Time spent with family can be nurturing and this may be exactly what you need. Home-cooked food and TV family favourites are on the menu.

Sunday 16th

It is a good day to reinvent something or to look at a project with new eyes. Think of it as a phoenix moment and see what you can raise from the ashes of something which no longer works. It's possible that you struggle with your work and home balance.

Monday 17th

A full moon in your family area can show where you are loved and protected. However, you may not notice this as there may be issues on the side-lines distracting you. Change is in the air and you can handle it well if you take family and work responsibilities into consideration.

Tuesday 18th

This is your chance for free speech that could be taken seriously. Don't try to be anything other than who you are. You may be applauded for speaking your mind or resolving a tricky situation. Uranus turns direct to help you come up with new ideas.

Wednesday 19th

You may need to review your responsibilities today. Look at the groups you're involved with and how their agendas align with your own. This isn't serious but will be a good exercise in remaining true to yourself whilst being part of your bigger community. This could be unsettling for you.

Thursday 20th

The Sun enters your social life and will help to throw light on your new group ventures. You may have the energy to influence the changes needed. This afternoon you may need to check in with your health or attend to mundane duties which could leave no time for you.

Friday 21st

Today, you may be able to persuade someone to your way of thinking. Harmony may feel difficult to achieve, but there's a chance you can win today. Money matters may be an issue and you could be finding ways of resolving financial issues that have troubled you. Women may feature highly today.

Saturday 22nd

Your true north or inner compass feels far away today.
You may need to give your attention to others unconditionally.
The greatest change can be made in the workplace if you aim
for fairness and equality. Think about others before yourself as
this may make all the difference.

Sunday 23rd

Personal relationships may help you to focus on other needs.
You must look out for messages, guidance or even dream
symbols to guide you. One last boost of energy is needed for
you to complete an issue regarding long-distance travel or
communication. Be mindful of how you communicate today.

Monday 24th

Mars enters your career zone and will boost your productivity
and status. You may find yourself with a heavy workload now,
but the right energy to manage this is available. If you are
feeling challenged in romantic relationships, this will pass, so
don't take it too personally.

Tuesday 25th

You could be a powerhouse of activity today and will enjoy
this. An air of optimism surrounds you and this is infectious.
Watch how your mood influences those around you. However,
this could be short-lived and by evening you may need to
unwind in your own home, doing what you love.

. . . .

Wednesday 26th

Mercury retrograde may begin to affect your workplace now. It's crucial that your communications are clear. Volatile energy can make it tricky to concentrate and you may feel that something is brewing and ready to blow. Stay calm and concentrate on doing the right thing. Check your position with shared finances.

Thursday 27th

You have an outgoing and far-reaching mood. This might annoy some, but be pleasing to others. Rally your allies and make change happen. By evening, you may wish to have some alone time, but find it difficult to switch off. Don't take this out on yourself. You could have your best ideas now.

Friday 28th

There is no time for dreaming today. You're on point with all your duties and steam through your day, getting everything done. That busy mind of yours is still ticking over until you realise that it's the weekend and you should be having fun.

Saturday 29th

Be very careful out there today as the energy is unstable. You may see control issues and power struggles going on. Watch what you say or say nothing at all. There's a chance that your temper may get the better of you. Back out of situations before they get unmanageable.

Sunday 30th

Today, a change of heart is in the air. This can be an emotional time where you might forgive or be forgiven for something from the past. This may not fit very well until you have had time to process it. However, you may realise that it's in your best interests.

Monday 31st

If you feel vulnerable today, know that this is a humbling part of your personal journey. Reflecting on recent events and grieving any losses is natural. Your social and interest groups will be your biggest allies if you need to talk about your feelings with people who will understand your standpoint.

FEBRUARY

· · · · · · · · · · · · · · · · ·

Tuesday 1st

A new moon is just what you need to make a commitment to your wider groups and communities. You may wish to do something powerful for a great cause this year. This will be commended, and elders will notice the steps and effort you take. Just don't sign any contracts yet.

Wednesday 2nd

You may have more time to ruminate and work on yourself today. Feelings of connection can be satisfying. It's possible to achieve a good balance between work and alone time. This may feel challenging at first but will give you the opportunity to make a game plan and write your to-do lists.

Thursday 3rd

Emotions are larger than usual, and you may be reaching out beyond your comfort zone. This can include inspirational people. Money making ideas may come to you, so ensure that you keep a note of these. Your work status is about to be levelled up.

Friday 4th

Mercury turns direct today. You can now consider any offers you may have put on hold. Things are looking promising regarding your true north. The energy suggests that you feel perfectly aligned and ready for action. Remember your responsibilities as there are people who look up to you for guidance.

Saturday 5th

If you can switch off from work for the weekend, then do so. Allow yourself some relaxation or use your free time to engage with group ventures. There may be a calling which asks you to step up and take on your new role. Group leaders are respected and followed now.

Sunday 6th

Your mind may be drifting back to work as there is a change in the air. This may bother you because it's taking up too much head-space. Let yourself wind down or you may resent being distracted. This evening would be a nice time to enjoy a long bath before bed.

Monday 7th

The week begins with all engines firing. You are ready to go and maybe a little impatient. Ideas flow through you easily today and putting them to the people in charge is easy. You may appear as a powerhouse of activity and plans, and you could be in for a reward.

Tuesday 8th

It's possible that you come up against a brick wall today. Normally you would have no qualms in breaking it down, but today you should find a less invasive way of dealing with it. Results may come late in the day, but you will notice how patience is beneficial.

Wednesday 9th

Quickfire communications will carry you through today.
You have your sights set on the future and know exactly what
steps to take. If you feel rushed or tired by the end of the day,
reflect on how productive you have been. Idle chatter with
friends or siblings can help you unwind.

Thursday 10th

You may have conflicting emotions today. Doubts and
apprehension may need to be appeased by discussions with an
elder or boss. You will benefit highly by the experience and
wisdom of another. It could be that you are being too self-
critical and not seeing your strengths.

Friday 11th

Listen very carefully today. It's possible that you are about
to get your new mission and completing on a contract.
There may be much to discuss or negotiate. This could be a
major new phase in your life and will require that you leave
something behind to make space for new growth.

Saturday 12th

Mars and Venus are getting close in your career arena. This
is great news as it shows that you are using all your faculties
together. Drive and compassion, active and passive, intellectual
and emotional all blend nicely to make you the best person for
the job in hand.

Sunday 13th

Today, you may feel like hiding away and being cared for. You may realise that you are too distracted and not engaging in home life when you have a chance. Use this opportunity to enjoy the comfort of your own home and family. Good food and company can feed your soul.

Monday 14th

You may not be ready to jump back into the working week. Fear not as this will soon pass and by midday, you could be holding your own conferences. Mercury has returned to your social area and can lend you communication skills in your group ventures.

Tuesday 15th

Be very careful who you upset today. You may have ideas that, to you, appear ingenious, but could rub up against authority. If you must make your opinions heard, do so in a respectful way. Remember to be compassionate and driven as this will be noticed by those above you.

Wednesday 16th

A full moon can highlight your romantic relationships today. This is a great day for love and creativity as Venus and Mars, the celestial lovers, have met. Finding your voice or your muse can bring you a delightful time. No need for a soapbox because all eyes are already on you.

Thursday 17th

Try to finish up any outstanding projects concerning your wider groups. You may have overlooked something important. It's possible you have an itch that needs scratching, or as an Aries, it could be yet another new project. Go within and do some introspection before making it public. Get armed and ready for criticism.

Friday 18th

Your true north seems unavailable to you, but this gives you a chance to concentrate on your career. Homeworking may be an option now. Get all your duties done and keep the evening free to do something for yourself. A new health regime may help to get rid of excess energy.

Saturday 19th

Love and relationships require your attention this weekend. A partner or influential person may be open to hearing all your news and even assist you in doing something for the greater good. It may be possible to find a partner who is like-minded enough to support your endeavours.

Sunday 20th

Stay away from unnecessary jobs today. A partner might be happy to go along with your plans, but you must also make sure their needs are being met. Refrain from selfish or selfless acts even though you may not perceive them as such. Let a partner choose some activities now.

· · · · · · · · · · · · · · · · · ·

Monday 21st

You could have an intense urge to investigate your love relationships deeper. Try not to be pushy and remember that everyone has their comfort zones, and they differ. You may give out mixed messages today. This can upset you and make for a sleepless night. Boundaries are important lessons for you.

Tuesday 22nd

Restless energy can make you feel over-protective of your personal environment. Alternatively, you could be reckless and make an impulse purchase which you may regret. You have big feelings which you desire to communicate, but it would be better to demonstrate this in the workplace. Check that what you do matches what you say.

Wednesday 23rd

Thoughts of the past may enter your awareness and get you clearing out some debris from your psyche. You could have an urge to free yourself from restrictions or broaden your horizons. Speed and urgency fuel your day, but for what reason? What are you trying to prove today?

Thursday 24th

Don't let your mouth run away with you today. Ensure that your conversations are clear and honest. Your mind may be doing overtime and confusing you and this could impact your productivity negatively. Slow down and prioritise your chores or you could find yourself backtracking or redoing tasks.

Friday 25th

You could have a crisis of conscience today as you feel that you are acting out of alignment with your life path. Maybe it's a case of cabin fever and you desire to get away. When was your last holiday? Your sense of duty returns, but late in the day.

Saturday 26th

You have a chance to show your leadership qualities differently. Leave work behind for the weekend and step into a different role. This could be parental. It could also be that your natural urges to do something out of the ordinary provide you with an itinerary for the day.

Sunday 27th

Today, there is wonderful energy for you to access and be your best self. You may be emotionally attached to being the head of a group or family. Self-control is important, as you could be called upon to lay down rules or break off old habits.

Monday 28th

Find a moment to pause your high-powered activity and observe where you've come from and where you're going. If you have an impulse to rebel, you will need to channel this in a different way. Listen to your heart and make a rational decision. This may not be easy.

MARCH
· · · · · · · · · · · · · · · ·

Tuesday 1st
You can do some of your best work today. Start from a place of calm and then let ideas come to you. When they do, they will excite and stimulate you. This may take up a lot of energy and you will be ready for downtime or introspection by evening.

Wednesday 2nd
This may be a busy day where communications are key. A new moon offers you a chance to look at your own habits and conditioned behaviours. You may be fired up and ready for action, but also be in the right mood to consider making small personal changes that will be beneficial in the long run.

Thursday 3rd
Something needs to change today. You may notice this in the workplace or your social standing. Your true north asks that you ensure this is in alignment with your life path and all that you value. You may have more empathy for struggles between the sexes and wish to help.

Friday 4th
The Moon dips into your sign and you can show off your best self. Putting yourself forwards and acting as a leader can give you the drive you like, to implement the many plans and projects that you have. Get an action plan together and make it realistic.

Saturday 5th

Inner work and personal development are doubly blessed today. You may get to the bottom of deep-seated triggers and figure out how to move forward with these. There may be something in your career which needs to be completed before switching your energy to your wider groups and good causes.

Sunday 6th

Mars and Venus enter your social area together. The celestial lovers help you to change your focus and use your compassionate warrior side within these groups. Change may be difficult if you are reluctant. This could include your money or possessions, and this may make you resentful.

Monday 7th

Watch your temper today. A hot-headed Aries may feel the pinch if resources are not as plentiful as they would like. Alternatively, you could find that an emotional attachment to these things brings you new ideas on how to declutter or redesign your living area. Use this bright energy to make a beautiful change.

Tuesday 8th

Take a moment to reach out to the future and ensure that you're on task to be your best self. Conversations may be sticky this afternoon but will become clearer by evening. Social groups help to exchange information needed to keep the peace and do the right thing for all.

Wednesday 9th

Your social life may be hectic now as there are four planets in this area. Teaching and learning from each other is more important, especially if you are new to this. There is great energy accessible and you can be optimistic and happy that you are on the right path.

Thursday 10th

Mercury shifts into your most private area. This is a time where you can investigate the depths of your own psyche. It may feel uncomfortable at first, but you will be sure to find pearls or hidden gold which need to be recognised and healed once and for all.

Friday 11th

Family time can be nurturing this weekend. Starting this morning, you may wish to plan and find activities that feed your soul. Chatting with siblings may expose some of those treasures in your psyche. Cosy family get-togethers can be great fun and make you feel safe and protected.

Saturday 12th

Many minds can come together and find ingenious solutions to money problems or enhance the home environment. Good food and company can make for a day of satisfaction. If you reflect on how you feel around your family, you may begin to do some important self-development.

Sunday 13th

Today, it will be glaringly obvious where your true north is directing you. You may need more patience or to look at things from a different perspective that will ultimately benefit you. It's possible that you see some conflict between the sexes or you feel the need for alone time now.

Monday 14th

It may be difficult to have your own way today. You may need to look at your wider groups and double-check they are in alignment with you. They probably are, but you may be having moments of doubt. This could make you restless or argumentative, so channel that energy into exercise and disperse it.

Tuesday 15th

This is a challenging day where you may feel caught between two conflicting options. All you can do right now is to pause and be the observer. This is no time for action, so refrain from using that Aries force and let off steam another way. Go to the gym, perhaps.

Wednesday 16th

Use today to check in with your health. You may have noticed recently that your high-powered lifestyle takes its toll on your body. You may need to think about supporting yourself with supplements. It would also be a good idea to assess your duties and try to offload some if you can.

Thursday 17th

Your head and heart aren't in sync today and there is no use pushing for results. Following your head and doing mental activity may be the better choice. The energy suggests that you can be more productive when plotting and planning money matters or creating change in the home.

Friday 18th

A full moon may bring your heath into the spotlight. You may see where you need to improve it or make changes such as a detox. People you rely on and vice versa will also now be highlighted. Make sure that there is equality in relationships that offer service to each other.

Saturday 19th

Romantic or business relationships benefit from sharing the same interests now. Especially if those are about making changes for the wider community. This may take some brainstorming and may be weighted heavily toward action. Aim to add peace and harmony and this will make for an enjoyable experience.

Sunday 20th

The spring equinox signals your birthday month. Take this time to pause and hold the tension within you before jumping into action. You may feel an intense urge to get rid of the old and bring in the new. Sex, death and rebirth are features for your consideration.

Monday 21st

Your self-talk may give you triggers to work on in the early hours. These may be regarding how you can sometimes act on impulse and be too pushy. You may feel uncomfortable at first, but by evening you may be able to reconcile this with yourself and sleep easier.

Tuesday 22nd

Remind yourself today that not everyone thinks like you. Deep investigations may be exciting, but can upset others. You could be working up to a full-scale eruption tonight if you're not careful. Broaden your horizons by considering others more and being open to another point of view.

Wednesday 23rd

Slow down and catch your breath. Both your inner mind and your actions are firing on all cylinders today. Mercury meets Neptune – your true north – and together they make a brand-new plan to enable you to access all the information you need. You may be more outgoing and optimistic now.

Thursday 24th

Moments of doubt and fears of rejection may creep into your awareness, but they will soon pass. The best thing you can do today is to stick to the rules and get all your chores done. Avoid unnecessary work and keep on task. You may feel better knowing you've been productive.

Friday 25th

The planetary energy is suggesting that you stay grounded today. As this goes against that Aries nature, this may be frustrating. However, use it as a chance to get jobs done such as personal paperwork, filing and managing your bank balance. You might surprise yourself.

Saturday 26th

This is an excellent day for making dreams come true and asking for what you want in the workplace. There's no harm in showing your vision board to those above you and tweaking things so that they align with your deepest wishes. You may have a trigger or golden nugget surface from your psyche.

Happy Birthday Beautiful Girl. 18 years old and yet sometimes still that lovely wee girl dancing around the livingroom

72

Sunday 27th

Mercury has entered your sign. Expect to be extra inquisitive now. Your natural inclination to begin projects may increase, so beware of burnout. If possible, spend some time with your social groups as they can lift your spirits and together you may start a healthy revolution.

Monday 28th

Love and romance are in the air, so stay aware of this. You could be feeling an emotional attachment to the work you do in groups. Responsibilities are tempered with harmony and you may be doing something simply for the love of it. Alternatively, a whole new passion is sparking within you.

Tuesday 29th

You may need to switch off today and process recent events alone. If you're tired, rest up. If you are peaceful, use this space to connect or merge with a spiritual practice if you have one. Be careful not to disconnect from real life and keep one foot on the ground.

Wednesday 30th

Great ideas can come to you today. Add them to the very long list you already have. These may be more in line with your true north than ever. You may have a 'eureka!' moment and find solutions to long-standing problems. This is what alone time can do for you.

Thursday 31st

Today, you wake with the knowledge that change is good.
You might be ready to tear down things that are no longer
serving you and make space for new growth. Your enthusiasm
is infectious, and people will be naturally drawn to you today.
Don't let them down. Blaze your trail.

APRIL

· · · · · · · · · · · · · · · · ·

Friday 1st

The month begins with a new moon in your sign. Make goals and set realistic intentions today. Your head and heart are in sync and, as an Aries, once you know what you want there is no stopping you. Mars – your ruler – aids you, so go ahead and just do it.

Saturday 2nd

You could be on fire with all the planetary energy fuelling your actions. Check in with your social groups as there may be an invitation you shouldn't resist. Try not to let work obligations get in the way of your free time. Enjoy a little indulgence this evening.

Sunday 3rd

The genius in you comes out today. You may have had a sleepless night with a head full of plans. Thoughts and ideas are flowing in and out of your mind, so grab on to some of them. You may have an opportunity to implement one of them today and it could be life-changing.

Monday 4th

A blockage may impede your usual speed today. The workplace may need more of your attention and you may have to put your personal agenda to one side. You may also need to check what you are committing to within your social and interest groups. This rest stop is temporary.

Tuesday 5th

Heavy energy can make you resentful today. An urge to move conflicts with the necessity to stay put. A day of connecting and networking via electronics can be useful and you may notice that this was a step you may have overlooked if not forced to slow down.

Wednesday 6th

Communications are lively now and this may lift your spirits. Although you can't physically act, you can see results and productivity happening through your networking. Venus brings a sense of balance and self-indulgence to your innermost world. This means that you can be kind to yourself now. Nurture your inner child.

Thursday 7th

You may feel happier about having to restrict your activity to online or phone calls. This may not give you the alone time you need to plot your dreams and visions, but getting things done is important and satisfying. You can feel good knowing you have done your job.

Friday 8th

Plan to spend time with your family and home this weekend. You could benefit from feeling safety and protection, or offering those to younger members. An overwhelming sense of empathy surfaces within you and you desire to have all your loved ones around you. Be the compassionate warrior and protect your clan.

Saturday 9th

You are showing your best self now. The Sun continues to put you in the spotlight and your natural inclination to lead by example is strong. Continue to have quality family time and you will notice this for yourself. People may share your ideals and will be easy to talk to.

Sunday 10th

Today, you may have a need to break free and do your own thing. This can be frustrating but allows you the chance to lead differently. Perhaps there is a problem that needs a spokesperson now. Could that be you? Find it within you to make necessary changes.

Monday 11th

There could be a lot of nice things stirring in your psyche. Pay attention to how this makes you feel. You may wish to connect with someone from the past or a friend you have neglected recently. This can be more pleasurable once you have got over the awkwardness.

Tuesday 12th

Challenges from within your social groups may disturb your good vibe. The trick here is not to commit to something that may become a burden later. Check that your schedule is not overloaded and, if possible, take time out to get in touch with your body. The gym may be calling you.

Wednesday 13th

It may be hard to differentiate a favour from an obligation today. If it makes you feel bad, ask yourself why. It could be that it conflicts with the time you require to take care of your needs. Solve this in your own unique way and a resolution will come.

Thursday 14th

An action concerning your social activities needs to be
addressed today. It may be your last chance to do something
important here. You could feel resentful, but will soon see
that when this is completed, you do indeed have more time
for yourself. Schedule in time with a lover this evening.

Friday 15th

Your private life is loaded with planetary energy. It's possible that
you find yourself floating in a dreamy world that is alien to you.
Take this opportunity to switch off your motors and go with the
flow. You could be surprised at what floats up to greet you.

Saturday 16th

A full moon in your relationship arena can show a completion
or result. It could be that you're developing a sense of
harmony that you never knew existed. This can give you a
great perspective on relating to others in romantic or business
capacities. Congratulate yourself on this.

Sunday 17th

This is a good day for you to deepen a love relationship. Your
energy and drive may be sharply focused on getting to the bottom
of something mysterious. Alternatively, you may do some detective
work around shared finances and find outdated subscriptions that
have expired. Get rid of unnecessary baggage now.

Monday 18th

You must be very careful with your communications today.
It's possible that you are probing too deeply and overstepping
someone's boundaries. This may result in a row, so tread lightly.
You have the chance to put things right and smooth over any
misunderstandings by evening. An apology may be in order.

Tuesday 19th

Turn your energy outwards now and explore something further afield. You may feel adrift with all that is going on in your private thoughts. It would be helpful if you find a way to ground yourself or get outside of your mind. Long-distance travel plans may be the answer.

Wednesday 20th

Your home and finances may be what keeps you doing practical things today. Are you thinking about a home or personal makeover? The time is right for you to beautify something around you and add some luxury to your close environment. Indulge in something that gives you quality.

Thursday 21st

Productivity can be high today if you stay focused on the job in hand. You may find that you achieve a balance between your inner and outer work which makes you feel good. However, don't push yourself too hard in either direction. Allow for some relaxation or exercise this evening.

Friday 22nd

Lovely energy helps you to network and possibly learn something new from others. This may be taken into your private life and give you food for thought. Surprise yourself by merging work and play today. A sense of satisfaction uplifts you in your personal endeavours and helps you on your path.

. . . .

Saturday 23rd

Communications or messages from your dream life may sp
you onwards. A conversation might trigger thoughts of skil
you would like to learn which can improve your surroundir
or financial status. Social groups can be entertaining, so dc
decline any invitations you may receive. You need to switch
sometimes.

Sunday 24th

You may not be in the right frame of mind to do much toda
This alone can be frustrating as you're a naturally active
person. Use this opportunity to have as much downtime as
possible. A duvet day with favourite snacks and TV shows cc
be just what you need.

Monday 25th

Although your mind is attached to your personal agenda, th
may not be helpful when dealing with your mundane dutie:
Responsibilities may be the last thing you need, but should
the first thing you do. When you're free of these, you have t
for your own things.

Tuesday 26th

Your spirits lift and you have may found your energy again.
It's possible to merge inner work with something around
the home. Perhaps you have decided that your environmen
needs to reflect how you see yourself. Your true north can k
mirrored in your surroundings and act as a daily reminder.

Wednesday 27th

Beautiful energy assists you now. You may be seeing everything blending and coming into line with your vision of life. Use this energy well and give yourself some credit. Also, give gratitude to anyone who may have triggered you into bringing this all together. This can be spectacular and you will be proud of yourself.

Thursday 28th

Today, you may receive a nod from those above you at work. It may be that you've been commended for doing your job well. This could also signify a change of status or a new phase in your career. Communications are easy and pleasing. Transformations are happening.

Friday 29th

Pluto turns retrograde today. This is also a sign that something new is happening in the workplace. The shift between old and new may feel uncomfortable, but keep your sights on the end result and you won't fail. Check your finances as there may be something there you've overlooked.

Saturday 30th

A new moon and solar eclipse may give you a few surprises. Money is highly featured, and you may receive a bonus or gift. Other planetary energies suggest that you have blessings to cash in today. This could be the right time to throw a party and celebrate in style.

MAY

....

Sunday 1st

The universe is asking that you give yourself more self-love.
Stop beating yourself up for things you haven't done. It's
important now to start a new cycle of self-care and dancing to
the beat of your own drum. You can still make waves and be
inspirational by being yourself.

Monday 2nd

Venus enters your sign today. This will help to ensure you
give and receive more love and beauty. You may already have
an idea of how this will play out. Check your to-do list and
research what is needed to follow your dreams and make them
big and bold.

Tuesday 3rd

You may feel challenged by something from your private
life that sneaks into your awareness today. Self-talk may be
negative and affect your mood. A trigger may also prompt
you into action but without the desired results. Maybe you're
making the wrong noises in the wrong direction.

Wednesday 4th

Put your dreams on hold for a few hours and see to your
duties. The energy suggests that you can be direct and
assertive today. You could be switching things up around the
home or making your outer world reflect your inner life a
little more. This could be a huge improvement.

Thursday 5th

It's possible that you feel your normality is being threatened.
This may concern money or your immediate family. These
issues could be under a spotlight today, but you have the right
mind to find a solution that you may not have previously
considered.

Friday 6th

You're on fire today and may feel invincible. If networking
is your thing, there will be no stopping you getting what
you need from other people. You may find that family are
supportive of your personal endeavours and this can give you
an extra push of determination to succeed.

Saturday 7th

A productive day can help keep the blues away. You may see
an issue of control concerning your status in work or other
leadership roles, but this will pass. This is the time to speak
your mind as honestly and kindly as you can. Stand your
ground in a conflict.

Sunday 8th

You may wake with a nice feeling, which implies that you have
acted in line with your personal path. However, this might
change as the day progresses and you may need to justify your
actions to someone who sees them as radical or wasteful.
Perhaps you have spent money unnecessarily.

Monday 9th

Stop or slow down today. You may have acted on impulse and
could now be feeling the negative results. Money may be an issue
and you might need to pay back a debt or loan. Be very careful
when interacting with elders as there may be a clash of interests.

Tuesday 10th

Mercury turns retrograde today. This will most certainly
influence your communications. It is doubly important that
you back up all your devices, save documents and learn not
hit send before rereading a message. Curb your impulses in
speech as you can be very direct and unthinking.

Wednesday 11th

Jupiter enters your sign today. His yearlong stay will bring
many blessings. Expect your world view to expand now. Toda
you may experience conflict as people demand your time and
energy and you desire to switch off and be alone. Be of servic
but also attend to your own needs.

Thursday 12th

A lover or business partner may show you how to achieve
balance in your daily activities. If you are involved in tactic
talks or scholastic lessons, ensure that you clearly understan
everything before progressing to the next level. It may be
tricky to say what you mean effectively.

Friday 13th

Look carefully and you may see an attractive offer waving at
you. Sexual attraction or home makeovers are on the agenda
This offer may also be financial. Look and consider, but refra
from committing to anything just yet. It could be simply a
mirage whilst Mercury is retrograde.

Saturday 14th

You may have an urge to deepen a relationship or an understanding. A golden nugget from your psyche may be surfacing and asking to be recognised. Do some detective work now. Look at your conditioned habits and you may have a breakthrough today. Old wounds can be soothed and hidden talents revealed.

Sunday 15th

Shared finances may need to be reviewed today. There may be outstanding payments or subscriptions you no longer need. Try not to get into disagreements about money which might erupt into a volatile outburst. You may clash with an elder in your interest groups. Take a step to ground a dream or fantasy.

Monday 16th

A full moon and lunar eclipse can manifest strange energy. For you, this means that intense feelings around money and partnerships; mysteries and taboo subjects may be the themes. Be mindful of how you are communicating today, especially in educational pursuits.

Tuesday 17th

A weeknight of love and romance might be in order. Your emotions are fired up to receive some loving. This may be selfish, but a partner could be grateful for the attention. You might be feeling exotic and wish to add a little culture to a date night.

Wednesday 18th

Something is going on in your private mind. A tsunami of emotions may be causing unexpected feelings to surface. Think of this a chance to heal or let go of this disturbance once and for all. Deal with it and don't try pushing it down.

Thursday 19th

You would benefit from doing an activity that feeds your body today. Exercise or yoga are favoured. You may have excess energ and need to use it up positively. You could feel resentful if you don't make time for yourself and only attend to work-based tasl

Friday 20th

A twist of fate may mean that your career has something to offer you that is aligned with your personal path. Don't commit yet, but don't dismiss it either. You may notice that you have a change of heart or the ability to release somethin you were holding on to.

Saturday 21st

It is important that you keep your eyes and ears open for any hints, signs and messages that can enhance your progress. You may feel like stirring up a revolution within your social groups, but keep quiet. Observe what is going on before sayi your piece. You could be highly influential in this.

Sunday 22nd

A quiet weekend to yourself with your private thoughts coul be your best choice of plans. You may have a lot to process and this will require your concentration without distraction If you are determined to confront old adversaries, do so after a great deal of thought.

Monday 23rd

Your engines are revving up, but as yet have nowhere to go. You may need to pay attention to finances or a purchase tha you now have second thoughts about. Don't act yet as there may be something you have overlooked. Something from th past bursts into your awareness and needs to be settled.

Tuesday 24th

You get a chance to realign with your inner compass today. This can make you even more determined to level the playing field, get rid of something which isn't working and lay the ground for something new. Your ruler, Mars, enters your sign to bring support, drive and energy.

Wednesday 25th

As an Aries, you are used to having big ideas. Today, however, the enormity of your plans is ready to be unleashed and made solid. Apply caution until Mercury goes direct as you could be going ahead without the proper research. Take a smaller step if you can.

Thursday 26th

Your social groups could be your saving grace today. Look to an elder or authority figure and get some advice. It may be that you are tackling new territory and trying to reinvent the wheel. Find someone experienced to guide you through this new adventure you have planned.

Friday 27th

Today may be emotional and you are likely to feel inadequate. You might have made too many changes in a short space of time and are now regretting them. Give yourself a little extra self-love today and soothe your worries with good food or company you enjoy. Learn to stop when you need to.

Saturday 28th

It's possible that you are feeling unstable and unsure of how to act next. This could also be a time when your best ideas and plans come from solitary consideration. Hard exercise or yoga can help to return you to your centre. Venus enters a zone that concerns money and possessions.

Sunday 29th

You may have a roller coaster of emotions to deal with today. Passion, anger, drive and determination can all be out of proportion. You could be regretting or mourning recent losse This is OK if you can also look to the future and see the new open space you've made.

Monday 30th

A new moon may be the green light you've been waiting for to set intentions to move on. Try to connect to this energy and ask what it is you can learn from past experiences. Your communication style may need to be reviewed.

Tuesday 31st

If you find it difficult to hold on to your true north, return to a friend or mentor in your social groups. You may learn that your outgoing nature needs to be curbed in certain circumstances. This could be a lesson that will come up time and again this year.

JUNE

....

Wednesday 1st

The love and security of family or your birth home can be supportive. Your emotional needs may be higher now as you could be feeling personally attacked or thwarted. Do what feeds your soul and gives you a sense of luxury, especially if you can do this in your own home.

Thursday 2nd

This is a good time for home makeovers or finding ingenious new ways of making money. You may feel like reinventing yourself and surroundings. Think about what home means to you. Express yourself through your choices of décor and let your wild spirit free. Be brave and bold.

Friday 3rd

Mercury turns direct today. This might give your difficult communications some breathing space. You may be required to redo something you attempted during retrograde. Challenges between the sexes or between work and home life might surface. You may want to pursue a love interest and get creative now, too.

Saturday 4th

Saturn turns retrograde today. You may find that your social groups need to rethink strategies or that members will disagree more. This will be a time to restructure what isn't working and find a new normal. Words of love may have the desired effect today, so say what you mean.

Sunday 5th

Tantrums are possible today as you may want your own way too much. You must compromise with elders or authority figures and find a workable solution to a problem. This may go against your principles but will be a valuable lesson. Considering leadership roles in groups will be a theme for y

Monday 6th

Your mundane duties and responsibilities could occupy you giving you an easy day. You may be willing to offer your services to others. Check your body and health and allow yourself time to detox, de-stress or work out at the gym. This is a day to be kind to yourself.

Tuesday 7th

A little self-care can go a long way and the more you receive the more you want. Sex, good food and the desire to be non-conforming can fill your soul. A mutual exchange in relationsh can excite you and provide the fuel for a healthy relationship.

Wednesday 8th

You may have forgotten about your own agenda now as something else has caught your interest. There could be a lot of messaging going on and a love relationship may be blossoming. Your productivity at work will benefit from you good mood. Reach out to a potential partner this afternoon.

Thursday 9th

Today could be difficult as you may have lost your sense of s You might feel that your drive and passions have been diver and you need to take a reality check. This influence is only short, but acts to take you outside yourself and learn to rela better with others.

Friday 10th

Listen to those who have more experience than you. You may hear something that you can add to your skillset later on. You might consider ending something, particularly in the workplace, but think twice. You could be being premature. Do some detective work before doing something that will be irreversible.

Saturday 11th

Getting to know someone better is highlighted today. A new love interest may be good for your self-esteem. Your adrenalin is being pumped to give you gratification in a way that is not usual to you. Follow your feelings and desires now. This could lead to a beautiful time for you.

Sunday 12th

The planetary energy suggests that you can meet someone in the middle. This is highly sexual and can be a turning point. You may be thinking about past relationships with money, luxury and things you value. If you wish to ask a personal question, be brave and go ahead.

Monday 13th

Mercury returns to your communications area and can help you with tact and diplomacy. You may find that your busy mind flits about and you can't fix on any one thing. However, you could be feeling on top of your game and wish to explore anything new to you.

Tuesday 14th

A full moon may throw the spotlight on long-distance trave
and communications. This can also show you what you nee
to know regarding your social groups. You may be thinking
about travelling to upgrade your desire to help others and b
selfless. Is this a short-lived fantasy?

Wednesday 15th

Reality bites today. You may need to get stuck in with career
goals. This might irritate you as it rubs against your good moo
It could put you in a gloomy place for the day. Just do what yo
must, as this low energy will soon pass and you will bounce ba

Thursday 16th

Your productivity may be low today as your thoughts are
elsewhere. You desire more quality in your personal life and
this could be playing on your mind. It would be helpful to l
at how you could increase these moments in your work. A
change, ending or self-discipline may be difficult for you no

Friday 17th

Friends and social groups may provide the entertainment o
downtime you need this weekend. You may wish to schedul
a meet-up with like-minded friends who can lift your spirits
Likewise, you may bring your own brand of joy to a social
activity. Connect with people you admire now.

Saturday 18th

Tricky planetary energy can make you uncertain or wish to
withdraw. You should be challenged by what you thought
could have given you hope. The best thing you can do is to
choose selectively from your friendship groups and enjoy o
on one meetings. Look for quality rather than quantity.

Sunday 19th

It might be a good idea to have a quiet day spent in solitude. You may need to realign with your true north and check that you are still on the right path. It's possible that you have wandered off the track and are unsure how to proceed. Your heart and head aren't in sync.

Monday 20th

Today can be more productive if you have allowed yourself to rest. Your inner compass is in sight and you can head towards it. A conversation may bring something to light and let you see with fresh eyes. Alternatively, you may have missed out on important information and need to backtrack.

Tuesday 21st

The summer solstice gives you the longest day in which to get active. This can be thrilling and make you feel like yourself again. Take advantage of the longer daylight hours to connect with others and have quality time. This can be enjoyable, and your optimism becomes infectious.

Wednesday 22nd

You're on fire today. You know what you want and go all out to get it. The energy in your sign suggests you have an emotional pull towards something that can bring you great satisfaction. As your ruler, Mars, is involved, don't hold back. Just do it.

Thursday 23rd

Venus now enters your communications zone and will add sweet words of love to your messages. You may now be pursuing a love interest by means of texts or emails. If you wish to deepen this connection, the weekend can provide the right energy for wining, dining and lovemaking.

. . . .

Friday 24th

Today can be full of surprises. Something could be stirring u
your passions and waiting to erupt like a volcano into your
awareness. This could be a rush of new love that will take yo
on a new journey. You may have unexpected reactions that ca
startle you today.

Saturday 25th

Sharing your dreams and visions may add a touch of mutual
appreciation to relationships. However, you must be careful
not to push too far and cross people's boundaries. You may
now see a glimpse of a future you desire for yourself. Factor
this into how you relate with others.

Sunday 26th

Take advantage of this continued good energy. Conversation
will now have the Venus touch and can uplift you in a way yo
personal agenda doesn't. This is something outside you and
not your own hard work and excessive drive. Allow this to flo
through you and feel what outside influences can do for you
wellbeing.

Monday 27th

Your heart and head are perfectly in sync now. You are likely
to wear your heart on your sleeve and give away your true
emotions in speech. Just be mindful of boundaries. At this
time your energy may be too strong for someone else. Temp
your natural urges.

Tuesday 28th

Neptune, your inner compass, turns retrograde today. This can be a confusing time and you may need to spend more time being introspective and mining for those golden nuggets within you. New perspectives are waiting to be discovered in the next few months. Try to be more flexible now.

Wednesday 29th

There is a new moon today that can help you to look at what makes you feel safe, secure and nurtured. You may be able to incorporate this into any new relationships, especially those you now consider family. You could resolve to offer and attract more quality to your life.

Thursday 30th

Today may give you a first peek at something through different eyes. Pay attention to what niggles you and makes you feel uncomfortable. This can be a call to adapt your current way of thinking and evolve it to the next level. Your personal growth will benefit from it this year.

JULY

. . . .

Friday 1st

Love and romance are high on the agenda today. You could
in a playful mood and enjoy communicating sweet messages
a special person. This can lift your spirits immensely. Childli
laughter may get you through the day as you remember how
feels to let go and relax.

Saturday 2nd

Challenges may arise and prevent your freedom this afternoe
Perhaps this is money matters. You may also have overstepp
the mark and upset someone important. Try stepping back a
observing from the position you're in. The balance of give ar
take may need to be addressed.

Sunday 3rd

If you are mindful, you may recover good communications
with others. You might be asking yourself what you can do fe
others unconditionally. Mundane duties may get in the way
of your free time, but at least you won't have to worry about
them. Check in with loved ones this evening.

Monday 4th

You may need to make a final push to be recognised as an
individual. This can make you too pushy, so exercise caution
It's possible that you feel resentful if you find that you are
doing more than others to make a compromise. Chats can b
strained and awkward now.

Tuesday 5th

Your focus might change today as your ruling planet, Mars, leaves your sign to concentrate on building your resources and self-worth. You could find that your communication skills are more grounded and practical solutions come easier. The necessity of this may be a revelation that you have needed for some time.

Wednesday 6th

Relationships may be extra tense today. You might not feel like continuing discussions that have been causing problems. It's best that you lie low and do your own thing until this mood passes. This is one of those days where you just can't seem to do or say the right thing.

Thursday 7th

Harmony may be restored today if you allow yourself to listen as well as talk. A lesson remembered from an elder in your wider circles may come back and help you do this. Personal boundaries are there for reasons and you might need to start strengthening your own.

Friday 8th

You may wish to explore every angle of something today. This could be in your love relationships and involve finances that you share. You may need to look at contracts, investments and taxes. It might be the last thing you want to do today, and you could be touchy and impatient.

Saturday 9th

Today, you may be too stuck in your thinking and are unable to accept another point of view. It's possible that you feel like breaking free from restraints. This intense energy may have you yearning for the past when things were seemingly easier. You may default to old coping mechanisms.

Sunday 10th

Respite is offered to take you away from your recent stress. You may feel more outgoing and wish to make a trip or do something radically different today. There could be something available that aligns with your goals and intentions for your self-development and personal growth.

Monday 11th

If you're concerned about conversations being misunderstood and causing tension, step back. If you can't resolve the situation today, simply take a break and do something which you love. You may wish to connect with long-distance friends or start planning a holiday. Do something that takes you out of your own environment.

Tuesday 12th

You are very much in work mode today. Your energy is grounded and practical and you may be able to plough through all your tasks in record time. You may realise that there's no time for dreaming and simply stick to the job in hand. This a great distraction from your recent troubles.

Wednesday 13th

Your work and home life may be in conflict, but you manage to work around this. A full moon in your career zone may show a culmination of something you've been working on. You might have reached a turning point and this calls for a celebration.

Thursday 14th

Change may be in the air, so you must be flexible today. This could be one of many new roads on your personal path. Get ready and scan the territory before you march out. You may wish to check in with your wider groups and see who your allies will be.

Friday 15th

A slowing down of energy may be frustrating for you and you could be close to having a mini tantrum. Sit tight and get advice from those who have covered this ground before you. A chat with an elder or someone in authority can be beneficial now.

Saturday 16th

This is a good weekend to do some introspection and be alone to process your thoughts. You could be thinking about how your sense of security impacts your family. It's possible that you're more emotional than usual, so go easy on yourself. Stress may come from feeling inactive.

Sunday 17th

Check in with your true north and you may find that you have support from family members. This can be comforting and will help you relax a little. There might be a conversation you need to have now. Is there something you have been putting off expressing? Reassuring words of love could come your way.

Monday 18th

Pay attention to your dreams now as they may give you a clu
to what needs to change. This may be a small change but co
involve your career. It may be that you need to finish up a
project as soon as possible and this makes you fret.

Tuesday 19th

Your self-worth may be bordering on negativity, but you hav
a chance to change that. Emotions and inner turmoil aren't
comfortable for you. However, today you can speak to family
and let off some steam in a safe place. Learn to laugh or find
children to spend time with.

Wednesday 20th

A struggle might present itself now, but you may notice tha
it's about your own ego. You may not like being told what to
or how to do it. Don't let resentment build as it will grind y
down to a place where you will feel stuck.

Thursday 21st

Slowly, your energy will pick up today and you could be
back to your usual trailblazing self. You may need to lead
as an example to family members and step up into your
compassionate warrior role. Find it within you to stand out
from the crowd and lead the march onwards.

Friday 22nd

You are fired up today and nothing can stand in your way. Unfortunately, this may get you into trouble with your social groups as you are two steps ahead of everyone else. Your inner compass is urging you to do what feels right but reminds you to look for other perspectives.

Saturday 23rd

Today, you may be buoyant and carry a spark that others are attracted to. You can be chatty and social, and make a great effort to catch up with friends and relatives. Optimism suits you and powers you through the day. You may walk your talk and be proud of it.

Sunday 24th

The weekend continues in good spirits. You might find that a little luck or a blessing comes your way. With Jupiter in your sign, you desire to expand your visibility to others and be noticed. Be careful, as this may also show up your negative qualities and expand those, too.

Monday 25th

The working week might begin with a bump as you return to reality and your weekly duties. You may feel this keenly and think that your luck has run out. This is simply a day where dreaming and personal plans need to be put aside. Indulge yourself this evening.

Tuesday 26th

Good food and company can make for an enjoyable evening.
Family fun and security can feed your stomach and soul.
Be careful though, as the energy suggests that you may show
off or say something you shouldn't. This may be a secret that
you have no right to divulge.

Wednesday 27th

You may be in just the right mood to power through the
day at full speed. This can make you feel good but leave
you exhausted by evening. If this is the case, spend time
connecting to your inner compass before you retire to bed.
You should end up sleeping with a smile on your face.

Thursday 28th

A new moon gives you the go-ahead you require to stand out
from the crowd. It may also pinpoint that a new creative or
love affair is starting. However, Jupiter turns retrograde and
may slow down progress or get you to reassess behaviours
you show to the world.

Friday 29th

Today's planetary energy is tough. You might want to run and
shout, but if you do, it may be frowned upon if you shout abo
the wrong things. Your bark will certainly equal your bite if
you persist in being direct and assertive.

Saturday 30th

A day with restrictions means that you need to stop or, at lea
pause and think of other strategies. These may evade you for
most of the day, but keep trying. By evening, you might have
exhausted all the details and triple-checked the facts.

Sunday 31st

Be very careful out there today. There's a chance that your mouth runs away with you and you upset someone from your social and interest groups. The energy suggests that you have no desire to stay grounded and could react to anything that is preventing you from doing your own thing.

AUGUST
....

Monday 1st

Where do you need more quality in life? You might have an eruption of ideas from your subconscious today that inspire you to act with immediacy. These may concern how you do things for others. They could also be about how you value wl you have and what you can give. ·

Tuesday 2nd

Explosive energy may mean that you're busy decluttering yo life, ready for new things to come in. Relationships of all typ are involved. Under this influence, you may seek to deepen a love interest or desire gratification.

Wednesday 3rd

Today is good for playing, loving and sex. Your creative ener; is high, but you need to consider how this fits into importan relationships as there may be an energetic clash here. Perha discussing boundaries and what you both desire can help yo to come to a mutual understanding of each other's needs.

Thursday 4th

Mercury enters your health and duties arena. This is the time to use your communication skills to express what you need in daily life. You might be able to go deep with this tod; Intense emotional energy may raise a few concerns but also alleviate worries.

Friday 5th

You may be reminiscing about the past and wishing that your life was simpler. Looking through rose-tinted glasses is not advised as it will colour your current reality. This may also cause triggers and old wounds to surface and make you upset or angry. Be as realistic as you can.

Saturday 6th

A dreamy day may be relaxing but will keep you in the wrong frame of mind. You may need to do something physical to get back in touch with your body and ground yourself. A weekend project may be the answer and can distract you from your personal struggles.

Sunday 7th

Today can be very challenging, so do your mundane duties then take time out for yourself. You may not feel like interacting with others much or if you do, you may find it irritable. Stay with your nearest and dearest and enjoy close family time with good food and fun activities.

Monday 8th

Focusing on work goals will power you through the day. An elder or person in authority in your wider groups may have another lesson for you. You may find that you're drifting towards your inner compass, but keep being pulled back to other things. Use this cue to do practical work.

Tuesday 9th

Power struggles or battles between the sexes may surface now. You may witness or be part of passive-aggressive behaviour in the workplace or home. Someone may make you feel guilty about paying too much attention to something, but you might be able to reason with them.

Wednesday 10th

You display an energy and power today that others may envy. You may be completely in control of a tricky situation and come away from it victorious. A family circumstance may come to a head today or require a last boost of love and harmony to progress.

Thursday 11th

It's possible that you're moving into a phase where you will be asked to step up your natural warrior tendencies. You may be required to be soft and strong. This will be noticed more in your creative, expressive and romantic areas. Children and play can also be themes of this.

Friday 12th

A full moon highlights what you have achieved or built up to in your social life. This could be negative or positive and will likely include where you have taken a role for a good cause. You may rub up against leaders and be unimpressed by your communications with them.

Saturday 13th

A head full of emotions to process can make for a restless day. You may be called upon to do regular weekend duties but also need time to switch off and turn within. This energy may cause you to speak before thinking that may cause some tension.

Sunday 14th

This is a lovely day for spending time alone and listening to your inner voices. You may align with your true north today and know exactly what path you will be marching on next. This evening you are ready for action and understand the need for changes and planting new seeds.

Monday 15th

You are perfectly able to handle any extreme emotions you are faced with today. They may not be yours, but you can empathise. Your communication skills may defuse a tricky situation. Think about how you've handled this in the past, adjust for the present and remember it for the future.

Tuesday 16th

You may put your unique voice into the world today. Practical tasks may provide solutions to long-standing problems and you could have your 'eureka!' moment. There are valuable lessons available to you today, so be aware and look out for these. Change can be uncomfortable but also necessary now.

Wednesday 17th

Take some time to look at your finances today. There may be something you have overlooked that is now due. The energy suggests that your desires to be comfortable may not be in line with your general duties and you may need to find different ways of generating an income.

Thursday 18th

If your self-worth is tied up with material possessions, you may receive a wake-up call today. If money is an issue, it won't be helped by being impulsive or rebelling and spending more than you have. Busy yourself around the home as there could be something you have neglected that now needs attention.

Friday 19th

You may be faced with a small challenge today. This could mean doing something you had rather not. A control struggle in the workplace may present itself, but if you slow down and take your time it won't be too much of a problem. Bring outdated projects to an end.

Saturday 20th

Today is best spent by making a lot of phone calls and messages to your family connections. You may notice that new energy picks up and this could result in disagreements or joined forces. Be a compassionate warrior and lead your tribe into healthy and useful conversations.

Sunday 21st

Your instincts may be to get jobs done in a rush and have time left for yourself. Unfortunately, these jobs and duties may take up more time than you plan for. Bite the bullet and do what needs doing. Check in with your health, too, as this may have been neglected recently.

Monday 22nd

A last chance to express yourself or say something that has been on your mind is offered. Be careful, though, as you may go over the top and risk saying too much. This could get muddled and you may need to backtrack or be clearer with your words.

Tuesday 23rd

Emotional energy may have you reaching for security and comfort. You could also be providing it for your family. You could satisfy your urge to enjoy good food and company by having a family get together. This may provide you with fuel for your next run of big ideas.

Wednesday 24th

Uranus turns retrograde today. This means that it will be harder for you to come up with something new regarding home and finances during this time. Be advised not to change anything that can't be changed back if you dislike it. Pull back from revolting and being the rebel for a while.

Thursday 25th

You may feel at odds today. You could find that you are looking back at the past whilst also being drawn towards the future. Stay in that place and observe your own feelings. It may be that you need strength to talk about something you are passionate about.

Friday 26th

Stay aware and you may notice a lovely sense of emotional satisfaction today. Your warrior heart can express itself and maybe make a difference to someone who needs to hear what you have to say. Don't upset any authority figures who may challenge you; be honest and open with your intentions.

Saturday 27th

A new moon gives you the chance to make goals and intentions regarding how you serve others unconditionally, your mundane duties and your health. This would be a great time to start a new exercise regime, although you may have to wait for your ruler, Mars, to give you the go-ahead.

Sunday 28th

It would be helpful if you can look at how you managed money in the past. Old subscriptions may be cancelled and finances you share may be cashed in. It's possible that you clash with your wider interest groups and may need to install better boundaries.

Monday 29th

Your head and heart are in sync and you have permission from Mars to get physical. This may involve a partner and could be romantic or sexy. The activity, whether mental or emotional, can lift your spirits or get you moving. Either way, you may enjoy the momentum it brings to your day.

Tuesday 30th

Partner time may need to be more subtle now. Even though you are happy to share and connect, there is still a part of you that can be quite selfish. This will pass, but try to play down your own needs and find mutual ones you can both enjoy.

Wednesday 31st

Changes and blockages may restrict your forward progress. You may experience intense feelings such as jealousy and bitterness about this. Take this time to look at how you can transform the old into something more valuable and useful. Find inspiration and use it wisely. Investigate all possibilities.

SEPTEMBER

Thursday 1st

Past activities you have enjoyed may come back into your awareness. You may also be thinking about the deeper or darker side of life's mysteries. Finances and joint ventures could also be part of this. Decluttering debris from the past may be something you could do to make a fresh start.

Friday 2nd

You could be in the mood for rearranging or switching things up at home or in your appearance. An urge for more quality surroundings may be on your mind. This can be done but with caution. Whatever you change now will be permanent, so think wisely before you take action.

Saturday 3rd

Connecting with a loved one may prove stressful today. You may have a need to discuss or explore foreign travel or higher education. This might be in alignment for you, but not for someone close. Let them have their own opinions and don't be too pushy about your own agenda.

Sunday 4th

Today is your last chance to use Venus energy to help you bring harmony and beauty into a creative project. The finishing touches you add today could make all the difference. Express yourself eloquently, but be very mindful of personal boundaries. You might feel pushed out of alignment.

Monday 5th

This is a good time to begin a good self-care routine. You may think about slimming down duties you do for others and allowing yourself more 'you' time. Alternatively, you could be offering your services in a way that enhances your personal growth. Be selective and don't overwhelm yourself with more to do.

Tuesday 6th

Today may tick along nicely as you simply get on with your work with no outside distractions. You may be using your Aries qualities of leadership for maximum benefit now. This evening you can settle down knowing that you did your best with a good sense of self-discipline.

Wednesday 7th

Social groups get your attention and you may wish to revisit a common interest today. There may be much to discuss if you have been absent recently, and you could enjoy the stimulus and pace this gives you. You may be the right person for a job that needs your particular skills.

Thursday 8th

Blockages and restrictions can slow your day down. You must think of these as a need to pause and reflect on the journey so far. Trying to fight your way through them will not help. As frustrating as this is, there is a lesson in it concerning your blind spots.

Friday 9th

You may be more introspective now. This is a good exercise and will help you process your thoughts on recent blocks. You may need to consider old habits and conditioning and modify behaviour patterns that no longer serve you. Remember to look after your health and to enjoy solitude.

Saturday 10th

A full moon may highlight deep-seated fears or worries you may have. These are showing up because they need to be healed or transformed somehow. Mercury turns retrograde in your relationship zone, so tread carefully here. Ensure that your words are clear and there's no room for misunderstanding.

Sunday 11th

Mercury may get you today as your mind and heart aren't in sync. This could be over-emphasised and make you feel under attack. Whereas your natural instinct may be to fight back, you need to let it go as you could be up against higher powers than you.

Monday 12th

Conflicting energy might make you feel uncertain. Part of you wants to run and this is possible during the day. You have enough drive and passion to do so. However, you may find that, by evening, you have been running for nothing or that the finish line is disappointing.

Tuesday 13th

That feeling of wanting to change your environment returns. If you can tackle this like you do your personal to-do list, go ahead. You can create a space that has more beauty, is comfortable or even luxurious. Just be careful not to spend more than you can afford.

Wednesday 14th

Self-indulgence may be confused with self-care now. You must learn the difference. Are you a person who feels nurtured by owning a lot of expensive things? Maybe you can consider your health and wellbeing as more important. You may be impulsive tonight, so be mindful that this won't get you into trouble.

113

Thursday 15th

You may be trying to justify to yourself why you have been irrational recently. This may involve expensive purchases which you believe are in line with your truth and personal path. You may need an unbiased opinion to make you think realistically. Try not to be too blinkered.

Friday 16th

Watch out for disagreements between the sexes today. With Mercury in retrograde, tensions will be high, and communications can get lost in translation. You may need to let something drop or call a truce. The Sun spotlights your inner compass and you may have a startling realisation about your dreams.

Saturday 17th

Emotions may now be too close to home. You could be very uncomfortable about doing something for someone unconditionally. You require payment or recognition. Alternatively, you may find that your health is suffering, and you need to step down and recharge your batteries. Be kind to yourself and slow down.

Sunday 18th

A family day may be the best remedy now. Your need for security and comfort with your loved ones allows you to relax more. Try not to leave a romantic partner out or you may find extra tension you could do without. Make today about someone else and not just you.

Monday 19th

Work and daily duties may fill your day and can make you feel productive and satisfied. You could be learning where the line is drawn before you are overwhelmed with chores. A new idea or plan may be brewing in your mind, keep stirring and perfecting this for a few weeks.

Tuesday 20th

Good food and company may be another thing which helps you feel safe and secure. Familiar things can give you a sense of belonging when you don't feel like going it alone. Enjoy this brief period as you'll be back to your warrior self before long.

Wednesday 21st

You may need to be extra mindful of Mercury's tricks today. This may be more evident in your communications and how you show up in the world. Take care not to clash with elders or bring a bad mood to an otherwise happy situation. Ego battles may be evident now.

Thursday 22nd

Although your energy and drive are fired up and ready to go, you may face multiple challenges. Adapt where you can, or you'll feel greatly disappointed with no forward progress. Make sure that conversations are clear and understood, especially within your interest groups or wider social circles.

Friday 23rd

This is a pivotal day and it's vital that you listen rather than talk. Partnerships may experience a turning point in which roles are discussed and evaluated. There may have been an imbalance which now needs addressing before any advancement can be made. Be fair and offer what you can without overloading yourself.

Saturday 24th

You may have to bite your tongue and do chores or favours for someone which take you away from your true north. If this is big, then you need to learn to say no. If minor, you could try explaining, without resentment, how it's not in alignment with your personal truth.

Sunday 25th

Have a day to yourself. This is your chance to indulge in whatever makes your spiritual, emotional and physical wellbeing feel good. It may be the day where the importance of this sinks in. A new moon in your relationship zone allows you to discuss fairness, equality and roles.

Monday 26th

You may already begin to see subtle changes enhancing your romantic relationships. Listen to your body today and see where you need to pay extra attention. Also, be mindful of anyone who may be trying to manipulate you into doing their bidding. You may clash with a big ego today.

Tuesday 27th

Tricky energy, thanks to Mercury, may surface in the workplace. Be on the lookout for mixed messages and passive-aggressive behaviours. This could be as innocent as failed emails resulting in work not done, but could also be more serious. Be vigilant and double-check everything before sending any communication.

Wednesday 28th

This could be an intense day that may leave you feeling exhausted by evening. You could be playing detective and getting to the bottom of a secret or mystery that has been evading you. Mars adds fiery energy to your conversations, and you may start a revolution in your social groups.

Thursday 29th

Venus enters your relationship zone. She may be able to smooth over any bumps and enhance the harmony now. However, today you need to be aware of how you appear to authority figures. You may be seen as an antagonist with a personal agenda. Correct them if this is wrong.

Friday 30th

You may be more outgoing today and desire to spend time exploring options for foreign travel or study. A partner may also be on board with this. Getting out and about further afield suits you and you may wish to make a plan to do this in the near future.

OCTOBER

....

Saturday 1st

If you are able to be selfless and consider a partner's needs, you may have a relatively easy day. Play by the rules and refrain from insisting on your own way. This may niggle you as you feel you aren't acting from your truth, but will be remembered when it matters.

Sunday 2nd

Mercury turns direct now. You might have a moment of utmost clarity or bewilderment. How you respond will depend on how you have presented yourself during the retrograde. Work and relationships still present challenges and can make you moody and resentful. Lie low and do nothing if you can.

Monday 3rd

Today you get a glimpse of your direction in life. You could be assessing past skills and talents and wondering how you can use them again. It may be possible to demonstrate one of these this afternoon. You could solve a money problem or a DIY project at home.

Tuesday 4th

You may be finishing up or scrapping a task at work. It's possible that you had a change of heart about it and realised it's not worth all the effort. You may have also looked at it through fresh eyes and seen it in a new light. This doesn't bother you.

Wednesday 5th

Genius ideas and solutions may be coming at you thick and fast now. These may come from useful sources you had previously dismissed. Lessons from your elders or bosses can be beneficial and spur you into action. New inspiration may come, and you can start networking on this.

Thursday 6th

Let your busy mind rest for a day or two. Go within and find your centre of calm. The energy suggests that you enjoy a moment or two of stillness before you rush back into the outside world. Your dreams may send you messages worth listening to.

Friday 7th

This is a great day to detox and declutter both your body and your workspace. You may sign a new contract or similar agreement and will need time to scrutinise it. Fortunately, you have the right frame of mind to examine all the details and look for hidden loopholes.

Saturday 8th

Your energy may be very low today. Take this as a hint to relax and unwind. Your inner compass is right there in front of you, so check in and see if it still suits you. There may be a small tweak or two needed. Follow your heart today and don't listen to your inner critic.

119

Sunday 9th

A full moon in your sign throws the spotlight on you. It's possible that you are celebrating a gain in status or a shift in dynamics at work. Pluto turns direct too which can help with any changes, new beginnings and permanent endings in your career.

Monday 10th

You may be extra busy now and taking advantage of the good energy in your sign. Efficiency and urgency are your middle names. An important conversation may be needed to determine your new daily duties. This may also be a medical appointment in which you get answers about your health.

Tuesday 11th

Mercury enters your relationship zone today. If conversations have been strained recently you may notice that this changes now. This could be a time where clandestine meetings or chats are exciting and prolific. Remember to listen as well as talk if you are getting to know someone new.

Wednesday 12th

Your day may begin with an emotional tremor. Something is brewing under the surface and it could be exciting you. Just remember not to push ahead at your usual steam with this as you could spoil it all for yourself. Boundaries are important now if you desire to connect mutually.

Thursday 13th

Today comes with a warning. If you must talk about yourself, do be careful that you don't overdo it. You may come across as egotistic. Use active listening to show you are interested instead of responding with a statement which brings the conversation back to you. You may need to filter what you say.

Friday 14th

Saturn has a lesson for you today. You must consider your personal boundaries and how you wish to be treated in relationships. This should be your marker when offering to be partnered. Treat others as you would like to be treated and all will be well.

Saturday 15th

Emotionally, you may begin the day ready to grab what you desire with both hands. You may fear losing something you have now come to value and rely on. Spending quality time with family or in a cosy, safe setting will reassure you that this item or person needs handling with care.

Sunday 16th

You may feel at odds with a partner today because your needs are geared more towards your family. If you can involve them or bring them into the family circle, this can be resolved. This evening, you could be involved in discussions regarding money and your values. Gather your dearest around you.

Monday 17th

Review where the line starts and ends before you feel too smothered and need your own space. Recognising this may help to avoid unnecessary tension. You may crave alone time by evening. Give yourself enough space to detach from the family without causing a scene. They will understand.

Tuesday 18th

A burst of energy propels you in the direction of your lover. You could be in the mood for play and creativity. However, be careful that you don't bounce around too much and breach each other's comfort zone. You risk getting a bigger bounce back, which you may not know how to handle.

Wednesday 19th

The energy between Venus and Mars suggests that you can achieve a compromise or balance in your love life. As always, you need to ensure that you aren't being over-enthusiastic about the wrong things. You may desire to break a few rules, but this won't be a good idea.

Thursday 20th

This is a great day for making loving connections the main theme. From a position which asks you to stand up and speak your truth, you may hold both masculine and feminine energy equally. Health and unconditional relationships will also be in focus.

Friday 21st

Look at what you value for yourself and what is important to you in a partnership. You may find that you can meet in the middle and merge these with nice benefits. Enhancing a relationship by sharing your personal truths can make solid foundations and deep roots. Listen with an open heart to what your partner says.

Saturday 22nd

It may feel as if your inner compass is far away today, but look again. It may be that it's adjusting to your new north. Having learned how to pause and listen, you may see a new level developing that could change your ways of relating to others forever.

Sunday 23rd

Venus is in the heart of the sun in your relationship zone.
Make the most of this beautiful energy and invite love, beauty
and harmony into your life. Saturn turns direct now too, and
this will make things a little easier if you have been paying
attention to his lessons.

Monday 24th

Your head and heart are perfectly in sync today. What's more,
this happens in your relationship zone. You could be walking
your talk now and showing that you mean every word you say.
Heartfelt commitments can be made under this influence.
You have a better idea of where you end and another begins.

Tuesday 25th

A new moon and solar eclipse throw a wild card on the table.
The next two weeks can be intense and life-changing. Romance
may get seductive and sexy, so arrange a weeknight with your
lover. Alternatively, spoil yourself with some self-care and
pampering. An impulse purchase won't hurt.

Wednesday 26th

It's possible that you get a visit from the past today. You could
be in for a big surprise, which may excite or unsettle you.
Remember what Saturn taught you about personal boundaries.
You should not feel obliged to engage in a social activity with
them if you're not comfortable with that.

Thursday 27th

How might you follow your true north out into the wider
world? This may be on your mind today as you're outgoing and
need more adventure in your life. You might feel like you are
at the start of a race in which you walk, not run.

Friday 28th

You may revert to old habits today and surprise yourself. This could be a childlike sense of unfairness and you may have a tantrum or sulk in a corner. Maybe you have been told that you can't go somewhere and feel grounded. Maybe you just need to do some introspection.

Saturday 29th

A frustrating need to get something off your chest may lower the mood of the day. Take a leap of faith and speak. It may be that the person you need to talk to has the same questions. Your conversations can only go deeper if you are willing to take the first step.

Sunday 30th

Mars, your ruling planet, turns retrograde today. Now, more than ever, it's important that you slow down. Trying to push against the flow won't bring any results. As an Aries, this will be irritating and make your restless. Find new avenues for letting off steam and excess energy.

Monday 31st

If you are feeling personally attacked or criticised in the workplace, look at what has triggered you. You may be able to identify your own weak points now. These are likely to be about how you're always two steps ahead of the game. Self-control is necessary to work as a team.

NOVEMBER
· · · · · · · · · · · · · · · · ·

Tuesday 1st
Don't give up today. Keep moving forward and making
progress, even if it's not at the speed you would like. You may
face challenges concerning your social or interest groups.
Question whether these are still in alignment with your
personal truth. This energy will soon pass over.

Wednesday 2nd
Allow yourself to have a slow day and let your dreams carry
you. You may be thinking about past loves today and this
could trigger old wounds which need healing or soothing.
Communications may not be going well at the moment, so
withdraw and have some quality time for yourself.

Thursday 3rd
Today may be quite emotional, but in a nice way. You may
have opened up channels to allow a deeper love to develop
with a partner. The next few weeks are great for investigating
your own psyche and how that can combine with a partner.
This could be quite a journey.

Friday 4th
You may see your inner compass today, but this comes with
a price. You may remember that this isn't the right time to be
acting on your dreams. Try to minimise your plans into bite-
size pieces that can be changed without too much trouble.
Big plans aren't going to work.

Saturday 5th

Someone from your past is likely to reappear today. This coul
up feelings you'd rather not deal with. Maybe you've suppress
emotions and they are now bubbling to the surface. If this is a
person in your present, open a discussion and resolve it toget

Sunday 6th

You may feel stuck in the middle of conversations today.
It might be that you're the go-between or mediator. This i
good energy, but you could be responsible for making the
decisions. There is another possibility that the past comes
to haunt you now. Tread carefully and be kind to yourself.

Monday 7th

Planting seeds for future use may be possible. Anything th
is on hold at the moment can be stored away safely. You m
experience jealousy or manipulation within your friendshi
groups, and this might also involve a partner. Remember t
put strong boundaries in place.

Tuesday 8th

A full moon and lunar eclipse may close the window on th
weirdness of the last two weeks. Today's energy is intense,
propels you forward and leaves past ghosts behind. Listen
subtle messages or whispers from your psyche. Don't act c
say something you may regret. Be an observer.

Wednesday 9th

You may be tempted to say something unkind today. Your
mouth could run away with you if you aren't careful. Trick
energy can cause a revolt and show you where there is
something wrong in your finances, values and possessions
Play the detective and figure this out.

Thursday 10th

It's possible that you run into trouble today with an elder or authority figure in your social groups. You may need to withdraw and have alone time later. This might be needed for you to process your childlike reactions in an adult way and discover why you respond the way you do.

Friday 11th

Today can be very frustrating for you. There may be some pent-up anger and irritability you need to express. Don't do it via conversations as this may not go well. Hard exercise, meditation or something you enjoyed as a child might be the answer. Try making messy art.

Saturday 12th

You may have a need for comfort and security from your precious loved ones this weekend. Time spent at home with your family may give you the support you need. Mothers and maternal figures, home cooking and safety zones could be the keys. Make a blanket tent and eat ice cream.

Sunday 13th

Stay in your nest today and work from there. This may give you time to think about things in a different way. You may be persuaded by a female family member that your responses were perhaps out of order. This may humble you and help you learn and grow.

Monday 14th

Step tentatively back out into the world and you may see that nothing was personal. This may have been an effect of Mars retrograde and you must now go easy on yourself. Self-love and care are something you should adhere to when feeling stuck. By afternoon, you may be more positive.

Tuesday 15th

Change is in the air and it may be happening with a close relationship. Try looking for more love and re-setting the harmony with someone before taking any new steps. You might feel anxious about this, but it will be beneficial for all involved. Remember to use restless energy positively.

Wednesday 16th

Emotions can run deep today, and you may feel like processing these alone. Your voice isn't being heard right now, take this as a cue to listen to the voice inside you. If you have the time and energy, you can go as deep as you're comfortable with.

Thursday 17th

Think about your mental health now. There may be something bothering you that is affecting you in more ways than you realise. Reach out and broaden your horizons. Planning a future vacation or course of study could be the right next steps for you. Let your imagination free and travel to new lands.

Friday 18th

Today can be difficult as again you're restricted from moving ahead with your true north. You may have to be satisfied with making all the necessary plans and research for when the time is right to implement them. Get radical and plant seed thoughts. Watch how they grow.

Saturday 19th

You may be tired of doing nothing, but there are things you can do to appease your sense of adventure. A partner may help to create a vision board for a future together. It may be fun and bonding to study together. Foreign languages, philosophies and cultures could be your thing.

Sunday 20th

Partner time can be satisfactory today as you may be able to meet in the middle and appreciate each other's limits more. A sense of responsibility towards your partner may be reflected back at you. This could be a turning point, which deepens and matures the way you relate.

Monday 21st

You may be working up to discovering something intense and heartwarming. The lack of action and speed could be deepening your roots and respect for a lot of things. Sweet-talking in the late hours can provide inspiration and excitement, which will be mutual.

Tuesday 22nd

As the Sun shifts signs, you may get the boost you need to put holiday plans in place. You might be thinking about putting down a shared deposit, so be careful that this is equal or you could become resentful. You may be reminded of being let down in the past.

Wednesday 23rd

It's possible that you're having second thoughts about something, but this is perfectly natural and is a way of getting you to slow down and check every detail before committing. Forget past experiences and look at this through new eyes. You're not the same person you were then.

Thursday 24th

This is a great day for making that commitment. A new moon in your travel zone occurs whilst Jupiter turns direct. Emotionally, you are completely in tune with this energy and double blessed by planetary energy. This is the green light you've been waiting for. Go ahead and plan exciting things.

Friday 25th

You may feel tired today and enjoy some quiet activity. An emotional overload may have caught you by surprise. Your adrenals may be getting the same fix you experience through your natural energy outbursts, but the unusual source, emotions, have confused them. Rest and congratulate yourself on using energy wisely.

Saturday 26th

Today, you may feel certain that your life is headed in the right direction. Feelings of contentment can make the day go without any bumps. Allow yourself to relax and lap up this good vibe. You may wish to make a note of it and recall it when you feel down.

Sunday 27th

You can make changes today that may elevate your status and bring you more luck. It could be that you've found an ingenious way to nurture roots that take a long time to grow. A change of heart or attitude may allow you to see things differently.

Monday 28th

Moving through your day can be strengthened if you ask for support from friendship and interest groups. You may be more outgoing and willing to accept what others have to offer you. It's possible that you're still pushing against the flow, but when you realise this you may back off.

Tuesday 29th

The planetary energy today can make you optimistic and upbeat. Wise words from elders in your groups are there to help you progress. Listen well and adapt what you hear for your own purposes. You may need to rest and withdraw this evening as mental activity may have drained you.

Wednesday 30th

Don't let poor coping mechanisms affect your good progress. You may default into bad habits today and feel bad about it afterwards. Don't beat yourself up; this may be a small blip where you relapsed into an older version of you. This evening, you may be back to normal.

DECEMBER
· · · · · · · · · · · · · · · · · ·

Thursday 1st
Keep a low profile. There might be a lot of triggers coming up from your unconscious, which can be unsettling. Your inability to make progress may be bothering you more than you admit. A battle between the sexes may stir up long-held grudges. Hold on to your personal truth.

Friday 2nd
Although your busy mind may have kept you awake, a desire to do what you can, however small, powers you through the day. You may be a little selfish now, but this is self-protect mode and is good for you. Taking on chores in bite-size chunks can make you feel productive.

Saturday 3rd
There is lovely planetary energy for you to do weekend chores and meet up with people. Reach out to people you need to catch up with. Your interest and social groups may have festive activities lined up should you wish to join in. Be as outgoing as you can.

Sunday 4th
Neptune turns direct today. This is great news as you may now find a secure place to cling when contemplating your true north. You may notice that unrealistic dreams and plans will fall away and reveal the ones you are most likely to succeed in. Check the seeds you've planted.

Monday 5th

Today may feel like another new start. You might have tackled some demons from your unconscious and sent them packing. A more optimistic outlook aligns you with a vision of your onward path. This could be more being practical and steadfast. You may now curb some impulses.

Tuesday 6th

If you have made travel plans, double-check that they are still right for you. There could be some doubts now as you take a fresh look at the value they hold. Communications at work will become a hotline for the next few weeks, so ensure you're meeting all your deadlines.

Wednesday 7th

This is a rare day where you can simply do what you need to and have time for your own things. You may notice that nobody demands anything from you and that your attention is perfectly on task. This may seem mundane, but you will notice the benefits.

Thursday 8th

A full moon sits with your ruler, Mars, today. Communications are highlighted and you may have a revelation or two via messages and emails. You may feel the urge for action, so make time for exercise. This moon may show completion of study or tie up loose ends and agreements.

Friday 9th

Settle in for a cosy weekend of feeding your soul. Family members, especially mothers or maternal figures, can give you a sense of safety. Alternatively, you may now step up as the nurturer of your clan. Give your mind a rest and see to your emotional needs today.

Saturday 10th

Women may step up and get the recognition they deserve now. You could be the one to highlight this. Restless energy may make you argumentative, but only in a way that brings out the compassionate warrior in you. Stand up for the underdogs today and you could be a hero.

Sunday 11th

Something may have dissolved from your unconscious and you now see it in its true colours. You may breathe a sigh of relief as you see how this can help you move on. You may notice a permanent ending as you leave this behind you. It's okay to grieve this loss.

Monday 12th

Your creative expression is what fuels you today. You may have a lot to say for yourself. This could be a technique you use to sort out what is in your head. If it comes out into the open, it's no longer churning around in your mind. Observe how you feel.

Tuesday 13th

Try not to go too far if you are currently making noises in some places. Your friendship and interest groups may not appreciate it. It's possible that you come across as a troublemaker. Say your piece and then withdraw for others to have time to process your words.

Wednesday 14th

Before the festive season keeps you busy, take some time to check in with your health and body. Is there something more you could be doing for yourself? You may like to declutter your surroundings, your office or your schedule. A healthy body needs a healthy mind and space.

Thursday 15th

The planetary energy is very grounded and practical today. This could weigh heavy on you as it's not natural for an Aries. Accept this as a day to get chores done. Making sure all is up to date will give you free time to concentrate on your own wants and needs.

Friday 16th

You may need to continue with doing practical things today. As much as you'd like to be dreaming up your biggest vision now, the time isn't right. Partner time is highlighted for the weekend, so if chores are done, your time is free. Achieve a balance between work and play if you can.

Saturday 17th

Going back to basics in a relationship could seem daunting. It may be that you have reached a level of understanding where roles have become seemingly mundane. Keep your flame alive by sharing duties and responsibilities. Just because a honeymoon period may be over, it doesn't mean you will have less fun.

Sunday 18th

You may be more concerned with group ventures than with one-on-one relationships. This could cause a bit of tension but will soon be smoothed over. Don't turn your back on something or someone unless you know that you can't go any further with them.

Monday 19th

It could be that you do an about-turn and wish to reconnect with a loved one. This may be a lovely reunion, or a mature realisation has been reached. Above all, you wish to restore the harmony you once had as you find it reassuring and supportive in love relationships.

Tuesday 20th

Jupiter bounces back into your sign today and will stay there for almost a year. There's no use in moaning about the past now. This could be another turning point for you and will keep you buoyant and optimistic through all challenges. Get busy adding to your dreams and visions now.

Wednesday 21st

The winter solstice occurs today. This is a time to reflect on the year gone by and give gratitude where it's due. You may wish to reach out to long-distance friends and let them know you value them. An invite to travel may come your way today.

Thursday 22nd

You may be feeling the slowing down of the season. It could be easier for you now that everyone else is winding down too. A last minute work issue may give you a chance to show that keen mind of yours. You may come up with an ingenious way of ending the year.

Friday 23rd

A new moon in your career zone allows you to set early goals and intentions for your work. You may be starting a new project which will take time and effort. Long term goals can be evaluated or set in motion now. Slow and steady progress will be required.

Saturday 24th

The excitement of the season is filling your heart and mind. You may have a deep desire to see that everyone is happy and informed. Taking a leadership role here can make you show off your very best side and keep you in line with your true path and purpose.

Sunday 25th

As long as everyone knows their roles and keeps to them, you can maintain discipline today. If you're entertaining, it could be you needing to stay controlled. Selflessness can be the theme of the day and will lift everyone's spirits. Enjoy this festive day wherever you are.

Monday 26th

Tensions may be rising today as you could be wishing to connect with people who are otherwise disposed. Perhaps you can check in with some online friends and groups. The holiday season may have lost its sparkle as you could be feeling too confined at home and need to break free.

Tuesday 27th

A time for solitude presents itself and you may accept it willingly. You may find a spiritual outlet supports your needs. Take this precious time to consider all that you have uprooted and dealt with this year. Congratulate yourself and look forward to watching all you've planted grow.

Wednesday 28th

This is a great day for dreaming. Your energy may be too low to do anything more. Concentrate on your true north and what you want from life next year. Your career, status, romance and quality of life are key themes you use today to align with your own values.

Thursday 29th

Mercury turns retrograde today in your career zone. If you have something new happening at work, try to buy yourself some time for three weeks. It may go against everything you have dreamed and learned if you rush into something in the new year. Be proud of any offer that comes along.

Friday 30th

It may be difficult to do your own thing today and this will irritate you. You may be dragged out to events which don't appeal. Keep a low profile if you must. Try not to exaggerate any bad mood as it could possibly turn into a hot-headed argument you could do without.

Saturday 31st

You could be missing out if you are sulking in your room. As the day progresses, you shed some heavy weight and come out to party. Spending time reflecting on the experiences of the last year will give you the space you need to look forward to the new year, and all its opportunities for growth.

Aries

....

PEOPLE WHO SHARE
YOUR SIGN

PEOPLE WHO
SHARE YOUR SIGN

. . . .

History books and social media feeds are full of pioneering Arians who have blazed the way for decades. From several American Presidents, to famous footballers, Olympians, politicians, activists, actors and YouTube sensations, discover below which of these trendsetters share your exact birthday and see if you can spot the similarities.

21st March

Rochelle Humes (1989), Anna Todd (1989), Ronaldinho (1980), Deryck Whibley (1980), Matthew Broderick (1962), Rosie O'Donnell (1962), Gary Oldman (1958)

22nd March

Nick Robinson (1995), Tyler Oakley (1989), Allison Stokke (1989), Gaz Beadle (1988), Reese Witherspoon (1976), Andrew Lloyd Webber (1948), William Shatner (1931)

23rd March

Kyrie Irving (1992), Vanessa Morgan (1992), Mo Farah (1983), Russell Howard (1980), Perez Hilton (1978), Keri Russell (1976), Chaka Khan (1953), Joan Crawford (1905)

24th March

Jim Parsons (1973), Chris Bosh (1984), Peyton Manning (1976), Alyson Hannigan (1974), Tommy Hilfiger (1951), Alan Sugar (1947), Mary Berry (1935), Harry Houdini (1874)

25th March

Justin Prentice (1994), Big Sean (1988), Danica Patrick (1982), Casey Neistat (1981), Sarah Jessica Parker (1965), Elton John (1947), Aretha Franklin (1942), Gloria Steinem (1934)

26th March

Louise Thompson (1990), Von Miller (1989), Keira Knightley (1985), Lesley Mann (1972), Stephen Tyler (1948), Diana Ross (1944), Leonard Nimoy (1931), Guccio Gucci (1881), Robert Frost (1874)

27th March

Jessie J (1988), Manuel Neuer (1986), Fergie (1975), Kendra Scott (1974), Nathan Fillion (1971), Mariah Carey (1970), Quentin Tarantino (1963), Mariano Rajoy (1955)

28th March

Nicolas Hamilton (1992), Zoe Sugg (1990), Alex Wassabi (1990), Lacey Turner (1988), Jonathan Van Ness (1987), Lady Gaga (1986), Julia Stiles (1981), Nick Frost (1972), Vince Vaughn (1970)

29th March

Lucy Connell (1994), N'Golo Kanté (1991), Dimitri Payet (1987), Fabrizio Corona (1974), Elle Macpherson (1964), Amy Sedaris (1961), Jane Hawking (1944), Sam Walton (1918), John Tyler, U.S. President (1790)

30th March

David So (1987), Sergio Ramos (1986), Norah Jones (1979), Mark Consuelos (1971), Celine Dion (1968), Piers Morgan (1965), Tracy Chapman (1964), MC Hammer (1962), Robbie Coltrane (1950), Eric Clapton (1945), Vincent van Gogh (1853)

31st March

Kamilla Osman (1995), Jessica Szohr (1985), Kate Micucci (1980), Ewan McGregor (1971), Angus Young (1955), Al Gore (1948), Rhea Perlman (1948), Christopher Walken (1943), Cesar Chavez (1927), Johann Sebastian Bach (1685)

1st April

Logan Paul (1995), Ella Eyre (1994), Scotty Sire (1992), Beth Tweddle (1985), Matt Lanter (1983), Chris Evans (1966), Phillip Schofield (1962), Susan Boyle (1961), Debbie Reynolds (1932)

2nd April

Michael Fassbender (1977), Adam Rodriguez (1975), Roselyn Sanchez (1973), Linford Christie (1960), Marvin Gaye (1939), Hans Christian Anderson (1805), Giacomo Casanova (1725), King Charlemagne (742)

3rd April

Gabriel Jesus (1997), Amanda Bynes (1986), Leona Lewis (1985), Cobie Smulders (1982), Nigel Farage (1964), Eddie Murphy (1961), Alec Baldwin (1958), Jane Goodall (1934), Marlon Brando (1924), Doris Day (1922), Washington Irving (1783)

4th April

Daniel Lara (2001), Jamie Lynn Spears (1991), Todrick Hall (1985), Heath Ledger (1979), Natasha Lyonne (1979), Stephen Mulhern (1977), David Blaine (1973), Robert Downey Jr. (1965), Graham Norton (1963), Maya Angelou (1928)

5th April

Rendall Coleby (2001), Lily James (1989), Hayley Atwell (1982), Timothy Bishop (1976), Pharrell Williams (1973), Bette Davis (1908), Booker T. Washington (1856)

6th April

Peyton List (1998), Rena Lovelis (1998), Julie Ertz (1992), Myleene Klass (1978), Zach Braff (1975), Paul Rudd (1969), Louie Spence (1969), Raphael (1483)

7th April

Ellarie (1986), Ben McKee (1985), Duncan James (1978), Tiki Barber (1975), Tim Peake (1972), Russell Crowe (1964), Jackie Chan (1954), Billie Holiday (1915), William Wordsworth (1770)

8th April

Allu Arjun (1983), Gennady Golovkin (1982), Chris Kyle (1974), JR Bourne (1970), Patricia Arquette (1968), Robin Wright (1966), Vivienne Westwood (1941)

9th April

Lilia Buckingham (2003), Brooke Raboutou (2001), Elle Fanning (1998), Kristen Stewart (1990), Leighton Meester (1986), Gerard Way (1977), Marc Jacobs (1963), Dennis Quaid (1954), Hugh Hefner (1926)

10th April

Claire Wineland (1997), Daisy Ridley (1992), Alex Pettyfer (1990), Shay Mitchell (1987), Vincent Kompany (1986), Mandy Moore (1984), Sophie Ellis-Bextor (1979), Roberto Carlos (1973), Steven Seagal (1952), John Madden (1936)

11th April

Dele Alli (1996), Toddy Smith (1991), Kid Buu (1988), Michelle Phan (1987), Joss Stone (1987), Stephanie Pratt (1986), Tai Lopez (1977), Jeremy Clarkson (1960)

12th April

Katelyn Ohashi (1997), Saoirse Ronan (1994), Brendon Urie (1987), Claire Danes (1979), Christina Moore (1973), Shannen Doherty (1971), David Cassidy (1950), David Letterman (1947), Bobby Moore (1941), Jacob Zuma, South African President (1942)

13th April

Josh Gordon (1991), Allison Williams (1988), Ty Dolla $ign (1985), Claudio Bravo (1983), Carles Puyol (1978), Jonathan Brandis (1976), Ron Perlman (1950), Thomas Jefferson, U.S. President (1743)

14th April

Sarah Michelle Gellar (1977), Anderson Silva (1975), Adrien Brody (1973), Robert Carlyle (1961), Peter Capaldi (1958), Bobbi Brown (1957), Loretta Lynn (1932), Anne Sullivan (1866)

15th April

Maisie Williams (1997), Emma Watson (1990), Samira Wiley (1987), Seth Rogen (1982), Luke Evans (1979), Austin Aries (1978), Samantha Fox (1966), Emma Thompson (1959), Roy Raymond (1947), Kim Il-Sung, North Korean Premier and President (1912), Leonardo da Vinci (1452)

16th April

Sadie Sink (2002), Anya Taylor-Joy (1996), Akon (1973), Jon Cryer (1965), Martin Lawrence (1965), Kareem Abdul-Jabbar (1947), Pope Benedict XVI (1927), Charlie Chaplin (1889), Wilbur Wright (1867)

17th April

Ryland Lynch (1997), Julien Solomita (1992), Medhi Benatia (1987), Rooney Mara (1985), Victoria Beckham (1974), Jennifer Garner (1972), Sean Bean (1959), Giuseppe Zanotti (1957)

18th April

Nathan Sykes (1993), Britt Robertson (1990), Rosie Huntington-Whiteley (1987), America Ferrera (1984), Kourtney Kardashian (1979), Melissa Joan Hart (1976), David Tennant (1971), Conan O'Brien (1963), James Woods (1947), Michael D. Higgins, Irish President (1941)

19th April

Joe Hart (1987), Maria Sharapova (1987), Candace Parker (1986), Hayden Christensen (1981), Kate Hudson (1979), James Franco (1978), Ashley Judd (1968), Tim Curry (1946), Jayne Mansfield (1933)

20th April

Mirandar Kerr (1983), Joey Lawrence (1976), Carmen Electra (1972), Shemar Moore (1970), Felix Baumgartner (1969), Crispin Glover (1964), Andy Serkis (1964), Jessica Lange (1949), George Takei (1937), Joan Miró (1893), Napoleon III, French Emperor and President (1808)